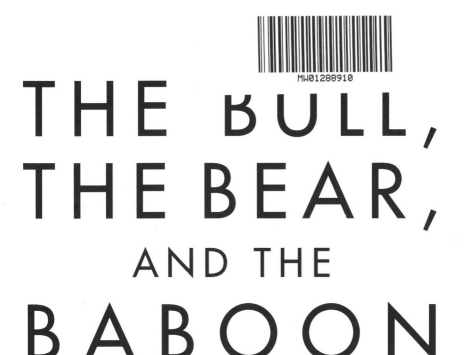

THE BULL, THE BEAR, AND THE BABOON

FX Lessons Learned the Hard Way

WINSOR HOANG

ISBN: 1484888987
ISBN-13: 9781484888988
Library of Congress Control Number: 2013909187

CreateSpace Independent Publishing Platform
North Charleston, South Carolina

This book has taken two years to complete, and it is gratefully dedicated to my father, Yen Hoang, with love and to my mother and my wife, who supported me during foul weather.

CONTENTS

Prologue ix

Chapter 1 The Phoenix Trading Instructor 1

Summary of Chapter 1 21

Chapter 2 Harry Dean's FX Trading School. 25

Summary of Chapter 2 40

Chapter 3 Everyone Wants to Get Rich. 45

Summary of Chapter 3 69

Chapter 4 Information, Disinformation, and Misinformation 73

Summary of Chapter 4 102

Chapter 5 Real Skin in the Game 105

Summary of Chapter 5 130

Chapter 6 David Versus the FX Broker Goliath 135

Summary of Chapter 6 164

Chapter 7 The Devil Is in the Details 167

Summary of Chapter 7 190

Chapter 8 A Thousand Live Trades to Discover the Trading Edge 195

Summary of Chapter 8 216

Chapter 9 A Tail Risk Event 221

Summary of Chapter 9 244

Chapter 10 Market Widow-Maker 249

Epilogue 267

Some Final Thoughts 269

Acknowledgments 271

Disclaimer Information 273

Computer-Assisted FX Trading 275

The Systematic Trading Solution 279

Introduction to CTS Forex. 281

CTS Forex's Systematic Statistics 283

About the Author 287

A Special Offer for Readers 289

PROLOGUE

Traders are risk takers, and good traders take only calculated risks. Many books on trading are filled with dense and dry technical information, and the advice they offer is difficult to absorb, much less apply. That is why I have chosen the storytelling approach to discuss foreign exchange (FX) trading, relating the (fictionalized) experiences of real people. The book has no graphs, no charts, no formulas. It is intended to demonstrate the pitfalls into which many new traders fall.

The characters in this book are real; however, their names and background information have been altered. I have made every attempt in this book to characterize these people and their experiences authentically. You might see yourself or perhaps someone you know in at least one character. The more you connect with the characters, the more you will take away from their stories—and, more importantly, from their trading styles and mistakes. This is a fictional book, but the lessons within the stories are very real. Pay close attention to the lessons offered in this book, as they may help you (1) avoid the problems these people experienced and (2) become a successful trader.

Common hazards in the trading game are greed, lack of discipline, deception, and financial ruin. The FX industry will truly test your character. It is like a vast sea of unpredictable currents that takes more than guts and confidence to sail through. Most traders will enter these uncharted waters under the impression that, with intelligence and willingness, they can navigate with ease. What they don't realize is that the majority of them are up against far more turbulence and setbacks than they could ever imagine. This book will open your eyes to what it really takes to be a successful trader and why 90 percent of most traders will end up lost at sea, never to obtain consistent profits.

Many of these lessons are based on my own personal experience and that of the people I have met. After nearly two decades and more than twenty thousand hours of trading, I have learned how to profit from FX. It was not easy, as you will see in this book. Ideally, this book will help you avoid the costly mistakes I made and achieve trading success more quickly than I did.

Although other books may focus on basic how-to skills, this book not only provides essential trading know-how, but also reveals the role your personality, your aspirations, and your subconscious play in your performance as a trader. It dispels many myths, including one of the most pervasive: that anyone can take on the market and win. This book offers what many trading books fail to address—awareness. Unlike books that entice readers with false promises, here I will present the brutal facts about trading. If you are a dreamer and believe that you can turn $250 into $100,000 in one year, then this book is not for you. It will not inspire you with the promise of riches.

In an industry that has become overhyped, overpromised, and filled with cons, traders will find it more and more difficult to find any real clarity and truth. The authors of most trading books only want you to stay in the game; what they won't tell you is why the game is so difficult in the first place. They fail to tell their readers that no single trading method or course is a silver bullet. Each trader must come to the market with an edge—something that creates an advantage when trading. In this book, you will get to know the characters' trading edges, some of which might surprise you. In this industry, you are competing with some of the brightest minds in the world, and they are often well funded and able to withstand significant losses.

It is easy to complain about FX trading's inherent difficulties. Instead of offering complaints, however, this book explores multiple solutions for dealing with technical pitfalls as well as disciplines and psychologies related to trading. My hope is that this book will provide you with hours of entertaining reading and insights into the market—insights that other books, software packages, trainers, tip services, and supposed experts will never give you.

What you're about to read may shock you and turn everything you thought you knew about FX trading upside down. Those who approach this topic with an open mind will learn a great deal. Okay, enough already—let's get on with the scoundrels and heroes, perils and rewards.

Winsor Hoang

CHAPTER 1

THE PHOENIX TRADING INSTRUCTOR

The first tweet came out at 8:23 p.m. "OMG, there's a person holding a gun on the trading instructor. It's live on the webcast."

"Someone call 911."

"Does anyone know where his office is?"

There was a burst of e-mails, texts, and forum posts. Shocked viewers watched as the attacker hit Harry on the forehead with the butt of his gun. They could all see the perpetrator holding the gun to Harry's chest and the blood dripping down Harry's forehead. They had been in the middle of a webinar presentation on how currency trading would change their lives, but all of a sudden, the webcast was replaced by a gruesome scene of violence.

As in hundreds of his previous webinars, Harry was about to close the deal and sign up more new currency trader wannabes. He would show them how to avoid the pitfalls and stay on the path to instant wealth. Like those before them, most of the students in this session would find out that trading could be a nightmare that offered little chance of success for the average trader. That night, the audience witnessed the compressed version of an overhyped and overpromised presentation on what trading can offer. They were hearing about the nightmare of financial ruin and life-altering experiences the "widow-maker market" specializes in.

• • •

Harry Dean was born in 1971, the middle child in a family of three. His father, a well-known obstetrician, had a thriving practice in the Naperville, Illinois, area, and Harry and his siblings grew up rather insulated in the comfort of their upper-middle-class Midwestern home. Harry's life was the American dream personified.

Harry's mother was a staunch Methodist and made sure that her children received a religious education and attended church on a weekly basis. Though Harry's father became rather well-off financially from his medical practice, Harry's mother had inherited a significant amount of money when her parents died, and their large farming interests had been liquidated and passed down to the children. She also enrolled her children in The Reade School, the most exclusive prep school in Illinois.

Harry did fairly well at school. He was not a genius, but his performance was not poor, either. He was a solid A-minus student. One thing he excelled at was sports. He played basketball and soccer and was elected the captain of both teams. Harry loved the status that this gave him at school. Five feet eleven, blond, blue-eyed, and well built, he attracted the attention of the prettiest girls not only from his school, but all around the Naperville area. He never lacked female companionship for very long.

Following his father's footsteps, Harry applied to the University of Chicago's premed program. Although math and science were not Harry's cup of tea, he studied hard and achieved a solid 3.8 GPA upon graduation. He had hoped to enter medical school that fall and applied to fifteen schools, but his hopes were dashed as he was rejected by every school he applied to. Crestfallen and not knowing what he would do to make a living, Harry got a job as a stockbroker trainee at a medium-sized brokerage house in Chicago, largely thanks to the recommendation of one of his father's closest friends.

Although medicine had been Harry's boyhood dream, he reconciled himself to the fact that this was not meant to be, and he began to enjoy the prestige the title "stockbroker" earned him, especially among the young ladies he dated. Indeed, the general consensus seemed to be that he was a young man with great potential and a real "catch" because it was well known that all stockbrokers were rich.

A year later, Harry met Jennifer, a raven-haired beauty with green eyes who had recently moved back to her parents' Chicago home after graduating from Princeton University, where she was a language major. Harry met her one evening when he and a group of his work buddies were enjoying a Bulls game at their favorite sports bar. Harry spotted Jennifer from across the room, where she sat at a table talking with a small group of girlfriends.

It took all of thirty seconds for Harry to get the nerve to go over and introduce himself after making eye contact with her for the second time.

Harry and Jennifer dated for the next year and grew more deeply in love as time passed. Harry found himself constantly amazed that he could feel such emotion for a girl. This had never happened to him before, and he had been in many relationships before he met Jennifer. For her part, Jennifer had dated many guys while she was going to school and had actually been about to marry one she had met at Princeton. The boy was from a very famous and wealthy family, and Jennifer knew that if she married him, her life would always be secure and that money would never be an issue. He truly loved her and would have done anything for her, yet something inside her told her that he was not the one for her and that she would never be truly happy with him, no matter how rich he was. She believed in true love first and foremost, and financial stability was secondary.

When Jennifer first met Harry, it was love at first sight for her, too. She felt that tingle run through her body that one usually only reads about in books or hears about in love songs. She was amazed that such emotion actually existed. When she mentioned her feelings to her friends, none of them could relate, as none had ever experienced the same thing. So when Harry asked her to marry him one evening while the two of them were having dinner at their favorite Italian restaurant, Jennifer said yes. Six months later, they got married and went on a month-long honeymoon to Europe. A year later, they celebrated the birth of their first child, Emily, who inherited her mother's beautiful, dark hair. Emily was the apple of her father's eye, and Harry never passed up an opportunity to spoil his little girl with all sorts of toys and other gifts. Two years later, the couple's second child, Rose, was born.

Harry could not have been happier. He was blessed with a second beautiful daughter, though this one had his blond hair and was very different from Emily in other ways, too. Where Emily was a rather quiet child, Rose was outgoing and cheerful from the moment she entered the world. Emily was more reserved and somewhat disposed to moodiness, unlike her effervescent younger sister. Harry and Jennifer were beside themselves with joy and loved their daughters equally, while celebrating the uniqueness of each. Harry often thought to himself that there was nothing he would not do to protect and support his little girls and his beautiful wife.

With his new family came new responsibilities for Harry. He now had three other people to take care of and provide for. This responsibility drove him to excel even more at work, and he vowed to himself that he would always give his family everything, even more than his parents had given him. Much as he did with his college coursework, Harry studied the stock market intensely and sought the advice of the senior brokers at the firm for trading tips and techniques. This was the middle of the 1990s, a decade of continuing prosperity in America. Bill Clinton was elected president in 1992, and his policies promoted business expansion that led to the longest postwar economic expansion in American history.

Despite Harry's stringent work ethic, he was always a bit superstitious, and this carried over to his stock trading career as well. Even as a little boy, he collected special things, such as seashells from the beach and rocks from hiking trips, which he called his "lucky pieces." He always had one on him and would rub the object whenever he felt unsure or nervous. This ritual had the immediate effect of calming him down and allowing him to think more clearly, which he found a constructive way to deal with apprehension and confusion.

Harry also collected rare coins as a hobby when he was a teenager. Eventually, he adopted an 1895 Morgan silver dollar as his lifelong lucky piece. Harry had stumbled across this particular coin while rummaging through the contents of a neighborhood yard sale when he was sixteen. He paid $10 for it and several other coins that day. At the time he had no idea that this coin would one day be worth nearly $80,000 at auction. Upon learning its value years later, Harry became convinced that the coin was truly a good-luck charm and, therefore, responsible for all the financial success he enjoyed.

Indeed, before getting out of his car to go to his trading desk every morning, the first thing he would do was pull out his Morgan, rub it three times, and flip it. If it landed on heads, Harry would trade a bit more aggressively that day. If it landed on tails, Harry would play the market more conservatively. Though it might seem ridiculous to most people, superstitious rituals are less the exception than the rule among traders. Each trader Harry worked with seemed to have his own lucky piece and a little ritual to go along with it. The most extreme case was Georgie, another broker who sat next to Harry. Georgie's lucky piece was a gold Krugerrand, which he would rub on his belly and under each armpit just before the opening bell.

As a stock trader, Harry began his career as a very conservative "value trader." This meant that he sought out companies whose underlying financial positions were very strong. Buy shares in well-performing, solid companies and hold onto them for the long term—this was Harry's approach, one he adopted from his financial hero, Warren Buffet. After all, if Warren Buffet could become a billionaire many times over following this strategy, why couldn't Harry? Harry knew intuitively that if you want to be successful, watch what successful people do and imitate them.

Harry was also a big proponent of portfolio diversification, and he always sought to balance his clients' portfolios according to their ultimate goals. Some were young and looking for asset appreciation in stock and bond choices and were, therefore, willing to accept a higher-risk profile for their portfolios. Conversely, others who were near retirement, or already retired, sought to preserve capital by investing in lower-risk stocks and bonds, where there was little downside risk, some value appreciation, and steady dividend and interest returns.

For all of his clients, Harry would buy only on the "dips." This meant that he would wait for the price of a security to "pull back" at least 5 percent to 15 percent before he would buy it. Being a "swing" trader, Harry took the long view by following the trend of a particular stock or bond. If he saw that the security he was interested in was in a classic uptrend that had continued for at least three months, he would wait for the 5 percent to 15 percent price pullback before buying it. This simple little trading technique that an old-time broker taught him was responsible for some of Harry's greatest investment successes. He had made literally millions of dollars for his clients following this rule and by adhering to the discipline of portfolio diversification.

But Harry was a relatively new trader and had never been through a full boom-to-bust business cycle. He failed to take into account that the market was in the middle of a historic upswing driven by the technology sector. This upswing had come about as the result of the confluence of many events and trends involving what we all now know and love as the Internet. At the time, it was more commonly known as the World Wide Web. Everyone was scrambling to get into the game. Microsoft's Windows operating system had changed the face of personal computing in the early 1990s. It was no longer necessary to memorize keystrokes to access a computer program, as one could now just point and click on a desktop icon that would open in a "window" on the screen.

Then in 1995, with the introduction of Windows 95, the personal computer really came of age. Windows 95 began the era of e-mail and fax modems through the interconnection with computer server networks spanning the globe, otherwise known as the World Wide Web. The information age had dawned. The potential of this new technology became apparent to everyone, and everyone wanted to jump on the bandwagon.

Telecommunications companies grew up alongside the personal computing community to serve as the link between the personal computer and the world at large. Information sharing began growing at an exponential rate as more and more people became familiar with the PC world and purchased their own PCs and software. This growth called for ever more "bandwidth" to accommodate the increase in data traffic, which led to a huge surge in the construction of cable networks.

By 1998, Harry had become aware of all the hype surrounding the "tech sector." His trading buddies had started to make huge money in this sector, and more and more of them seemed to be over allocating their portfolios with tech stocks. It was hard to dispute the obvious success they were enjoying—it was not uncommon for their investments to double or triple in a six-month period. Many of the companies in which they invested were small or start-ups and had very little in the way of assets other than the initial public offering money that got them off the ground, so a new metric became fashionable for the professional investor to use when evaluating such stocks. The key seemed to be what a tech company's "burn rate" was. The burn rate was the amount of time it would take a start-up company to eat through its capital before it would start to show profits. If a company's burn rate was sufficient for it to gain a foothold in its market and, therefore, start to make a profit before its money ran out, it was a good bet.

Harry could not quite figure out this concept. How could the markets be supporting these companies, which had no history of profit making or dividends, with such high valuations? Harry had never seen a market like this before. The business press called it the "new economy" and seemed to look down on the poor commoners who just were not able to get their heads around its new math. Harry was certain it was a fad when the mantra of the day for companies became "built to flip."

Much of the tech-sector explosion was due to a major design flaw in computer software and hardware that had recently come to light. Before 1990, many software programmers and manufacturers of hardware had used a two-digit code to stand for the year in dates. This practice led to a big problem because the year 2000 was fast approaching. It was widely believed that computers that had not been updated with newer features would think the year 2000 was, in reality, 1900. Panic spread throughout business and industry that malfunctioning computers would lead to all manner of disasters, such as planes falling out of the sky, a loss of worldwide financial information, and the inadvertent launch of nuclear missiles. It would surely be the end of the modern world.

Though most of this fear was unfounded, there was a legitimate need to fix the problem. A company had to become "Y2K-compliant" if it wanted to stay in business. Otherwise, no one would risk doing business with it. Compliance, of course, led to a huge increase in all types of computer-related improvements and upgrades. Companies spent enormous amounts of money on new computer equipment and software. Only the latest Y2K-compliant technology would do the trick, and it was expensive, as demand outstripped supply. Between 1998 and 2000, IT departments around the world became the center of their corporate universes. Never before had information technology managers held such power and been given such freedom to acquire what they thought their companies should have.

As months went on, Harry could no longer justify strict adherence to his value investment philosophy. His trading buddies laughed openly at him for being such an old fogy. Value trading's time had come and gone, they said. The real money was in seeing the future, and that future was in the tech world. Indeed, it was hard to argue with this logic as tech stocks outperformed traditional companies by five to ten times on average. If one was not heavy in tech stocks, clients would leave because they all had friends who were making a killing in the tech sector.

More and more of Harry's trading colleagues, and his clients, were pushing him to take risks that he never would have dreamed of six months before. These tech stocks flew in the face of all that Harry held dear and had been trained to avoid, yet the money being made just could not be overlooked. So Harry found himself investing in this brand-new market more and more. Every day that Harry invested in the tech sector, he made more money for his clients and himself. He even began selling off his favorite standby stocks with companies such as Exxon and Procter & Gamble in favor of tech companies such as Dell and HP and many smaller Internet companies—companies that did not produce hardware, but some variation of software or web support to be used with the PC.

Hardware manufacturers such as Dell and HP and their competitors were producing Y2K-compliant machines at breakneck speed to meet the new demand. Software companies were also designing Y2K-compliant programs to be used in the new hardware. This led to a huge upturn in business in the tech sector starting around 1998. Companies like Dell, HP, etc., were cranking out new machines loaded with Y2K-compliant software at an astonishing rate. Many companies and individuals saw this as an opportunity to upgrade their systems.

Chip makers and manufacturers of modems, monitors, CD-ROMs, and everything else relating to the PC saw massive increases in demand and sales. Companies related to the computer industry in any way made money as well, from cardboard companies that made the boxes the PCs were shipped in to chemical companies that created the plastics used in the computers and everything in between.

In this new information age, the hardware and software companies and the telecommunications companies that were supporting them were riding high, and the stock markets reflected that. Any company remotely related to the information sector was making money. Venture capitalists were on a constant lookout for the next Dell, HP, or Microsoft. And this led to the "dot-com bubble" that created vast increases in market capitalization trading on the NASDAQ stock index. NASDAQ doubled and then doubled again. Investment fever spread as the stock prices of start-up companies doubled, tripled, and quadrupled.

This was the market that Harry Dean found himself in. From 1995 to 2000, Harry was making nearly $500,000 a year. He had become so successful that he no longer needed to prospect for clients; his existing clients referred their friends and family members to him. By 1998, Harry was a senior broker at one of the largest brokerage houses in the country. He lived in an exclusive Chicago suburb with his beautiful wife and two adorable girls. The family had more than enough money to enjoy life to the fullest, going on vacations to the South of France and Tahiti. He drove a Porsche 911 Turbo, and his wife drove the newest Mercedes 500.

Business was so good, Harry bet his wife that he would bring home over $1 million by the end of 1999. If he lost the bet, he would have to buy her a new diamond ring worth at least $200,000. If he won, he could buy himself the Lamborghini Diablo that he had always wanted. At the end of that year, Harry made $1.5 million and bought both the new Diablo and a new ring for his wife.

The kids were enrolled in a preppy nursery school that some said was harder to get into than Harvard. His wife shopped at Neiman Marcus, Saks, and Lord & Taylor. Harry belonged to one of the most exclusive golf clubs in the Chicago metro area, where he always played eighteen holes on Sunday. His country club membership would often provide him with new clients, and he became known at the club as the go-to broker.

Things were very good indeed for Harry Dean, but for some reason, he could not seem to get rid of the nervous feeling he felt in his stomach every morning when he walked from his car into the brokerage house. He found himself rubbing his Morgan silver dollar more and more throughout the day, but he just could not get rid of the feeling deep in his gut that something was wrong. Something was very wrong, but he just could not put his finger on it. He was getting less and less sleep at night. He would frequently wake up in a cold sweat from dreams in which he saw himself losing not only all of his clients' money, but his family's as well. Why was he feeling this way when he was making so much money? Was his new investment strategy wrong? How could he be wrong when he was just doing what everyone else in the market was doing? Surely everyone could not be wrong, especially not when the facts supported his new investment focus.

Any new company with any association with the tech sector could, and often did, bring an initial public offering and make its founders instant millionaires. Cities all over the United States wanted to become the next Silicon Valley and offered start-up tech companies all sorts of development incentives, from tax abatements to infrastructure support and construction to development loans. The market was on fire.

As the months rolled on, Harry became more and more nervous, to the point that he had to seek medical advice about his anxiety attacks. One day, while watching his kids play at the local park, he suddenly felt an agonizing tightness in his chest, and his breathing became difficult. Oh, no, he thought, I can't die now. My kids are too little and need me so much; how can I leave them now? What will happen to Jen? After a few hours, his symptoms went away, and Harry would attribute them to side effects from the Mexican food he ate for lunch, maybe a hot pepper or some other exotic ingredient that his body was not used to. Probably just an allergic reaction, he thought.

A week later, while on a call with a client in one of his firm's conference rooms, he felt the pain again. This time, it seemed like his heart was being squeezed in a vice. His breathing became difficult, and his eyes began to lose focus. As he sat in the conference room painfully gasping for air, his colleagues assumed he was having a heart attack. They immediately called an ambulance that rushed him to the hospital. There, after a battery of tests, the attending physician could find nothing wrong with Harry other than the classic symptoms of a panic attack. After giving Harry a prescription for Xanax, an antianxiety medication, and providing a referral to a psychiatrist, the doctor discharged him to the waiting arms of his very worried wife.

Harry contacted the psychiatrist to begin therapy and kept up with his daily Xanax dosage, but neither eliminated his anxiety. Both lessened his symptoms, but they did not remove them completely. Harry became convinced that only more Xanax would work for him and eventually get him back to his old self, but his psychiatrist would not increase the dosage and warned Harry that Xanax was addictive. Harry found another psychiatrist and got another prescription for Xanax.

Harry was now taking twice the recommended daily maximum of this drug. At that level, the medication was working, but Harry turned into a total zombie. Under that much medication, he was in a fog most of the day. The only time he was clear-headed was first thing in the morning when he woke up. His wife and kids noticed the change in him and became extremely worried but did not know what to do—after all, he was being monitored by doctors. They knew best, didn't they?

Then the inevitable happened. The tech market bubble began to burst in early 2000. Once the flood of system upgrades was completed and the potential Y2K threat had passed, the market for technical goods reached its saturation point. Orders for new equipment and software began to slow down. Many business and retail consumers had upgraded their PCs and stopped buying new ones. By the end of 2000, the downturn in the tech sector reached a point that the NASDAQ lost 75 percent of its value, and nearly $1 trillion in market capitalization just evaporated.

Harry's biggest nightmare was starting to come to life. All of the tech stocks that he owned and had purchased on behalf of his clients began losing value. It started slowly at first, but as the weeks went on, the bad news just continued. Harry tried every trick he could think of. At first, he thought he could just buy more on the dips and make up for the losses when the market regained some traction and corrected, but it never did. Even his lucky Morgan silver dollar did nothing to stop the bloodletting.

In stock trading, the brokerages allow the investors to borrow money to buy security. In margin accounts, an investor puts down 50 percent of the value of a purchase and borrows the rest from the broker. The broker charges the investor for the borrowed money and uses the securities for collateral. The margin accounts Harry had set up for himself and his clients were making a great deal of money when the high-tech stocks skyrocketed. With increasing profits in these accounts, more money was borrowed to compound the winnings. As the stocks headed south, his accounts were getting margin called. Harry found himself owing the bank $4.3 million. Margin trading used the power of borrowed money to magnify his winnings, but it also amplified his losses once the market underperformed.

His clients, sensing that the market was beginning to turn against them, swamped Harry with sell orders. Harry, never having faced a falling market before, could do little to stop his clients' losses. By the end of 2000, Harry was broke, as were most of his clients, who blamed him for their losses. Jennifer slowly started to realize that their ideal life had come completely undone. They were forced to sell their beautiful home, and they could no longer afford their girls' private school nor their expensive cars and lifestyle. Within a few more months, when it failed to sell, their house was in foreclosure, and they were forced to vacate. Harry even had to part with his lucky Morgan silver dollar.

With nowhere else to go, Harry persuaded his parents to take them in since they had a large house. He and his little family found themselves living back where he started, in Naperville. The brokerage business was now closed to Harry because the market was contracting, and no firms were hiring. To make money for basic necessities, he took a job with an insurance company as a sales trainee, but this barely covered his car expenses, much less provided a living for his family. He was so desperate that he had to rely on financial help from his father to make ends meet.

Harry found himself creeping into a really dark place. As Sylvia Plath once aptly described it, "[W]herever I was…I'd be sitting under the same glass bell jar, stewing in my own sour air." Harry was in that bell jar, feeling withdrawn, isolated, and lacking any interest in life. He struggled to find meaning in his new job, and everything just paled in comparison to the luxury he had enjoyed during his stockbroker days. He was gradually losing the will and the drive to get through each day. Everything was bland and colorless.

Depression descended on Harry. He had a wife and family, and if he could not make himself happy, how could he even attempt to make them happy? Harry expected people to be understanding and compassionate in the face of his depression, but what usually happened was that people grew frustrated and impatient with him, and that compounded the depression. This was exactly what happened with Harry and Jennifer. Their marriage was plagued with tension and negative energy. The strain was becoming agonizing, and he and Jennifer were fighting more and more each day. Secretly, Jennifer kicked herself for not marrying the boy she had dated at Princeton. This would never have happened if she had married him—a recurring thought that haunted her daily. Harry sensed she had been thinking about all the other opportunities she had passed up to be with him. He knew she could see him slipping ever deeper into depression, and that added salt to his wounds. Trading had made Harry feel like a king, and now he was one step away from being a beggar, living on the street.

It was during this dark period that Harry noticed something going on in the investment community. Despite being out of the business, he had remained connected mainly by reading the *Wall Street Journal*, which he got at the local public library, generally a day old. The federal government under President Clinton had deregulated something called the commodity futures market in 1999, he learned, and a new foreign exchange market was now available to the small investor. Before deregulation, only large international banks and corporations invested in this market, and it was considered closed to all but the "big boys."

This seemed to Harry to be a way to get back in the game. Could the foreign exchange market get him out of the bell jar and bring the color back to his life? He read every book he could find on this "FX" thing. He attended seminars held by FX brokerage houses, which had sprung up like mushrooms after a summer's rain. He even became an avid reader of FX website forums, where he learned about numerous trading systems, each of which promised to turn an investment of as little as $500 into $5,000 in as little as three months. How could this be true? He questioned the legitimacy of the statements but at the same time was fascinated by the tremendous potential FX trading offered—particularly if one used a brokerage that offered 100:1 leverage, and some were even offering 400:1 leverage. Trading on margin or leverage is the common attraction of the FX market. One can purchase $100,000 EUR/USD position with a $250 account balance (400:1 leverage). Harry shivered, recalling his riches-to-rags margin account experience when he was using only 2:1 leverage.

Reviewing his investing career further, and trying to contrast the stock market where he came from with this new FX market,

Harry realized that during his five years of stock trading, approximately 80 percent of all the trades he made for himself and his clients were "buy-side" trades, which depended on the underlying stock continuing to increase in value to create a profit. Only on the very rare occasion when Harry had some information about a stock not doing well did he short a stock.

It was then that Harry realized that for the five years he had been trading stocks, he had done so in a market that was going in only one direction: up. Harry then started looking at some historical stock market data, and what he learned was that the stock markets differed considerably from the FX market, and the key difference seemed to be that the stock markets tended to trend for years in either an upward or downward direction. Harry had gotten into stock trading at the midpoint of a long bull market.

Harry then looked at the FX market and saw the vast difference in the direction and speed at which it could go. In the span of an hour, the price of an FX spot market could change wildly from an uptrend to a downtrend. This volatility presented the investor with substantial risk, but also substantial reward. Learning to determine the direction of the FX spot market was absolutely critical for trading success. Moreover, traders must constantly switch from a buy trades bias to a sell trades bias.

Harry was smitten. FX seemed to him the ticket back to the good life—his old life, the life he had before, with the big house, fancy cars, and expensive schools. Harry genuinely believed that FX could get his family their old life back, so he told Jennifer that he wanted to invest their small savings in opening an FX trading account. This idea did not go over well. In fact, Jennifer was so put off by the whole stock market disaster that she told Harry if he started FX trading, their marriage was over. Not only would she leave him, but she'd take the kids to live with her parents in

Chicago. Jennifer would prefer Harry try to make it in the insurance business, which seemed to her much more stable, than for him to enter the highly unstable world of the markets once again.

Harry couldn't bear the thought of losing his family, and yet he was still strangely compelled to get involved in the FX markets. How could he participate in this new and fascinating marketplace and still keep hold of his family, while continuing to pursue the insurance business? After several more months of pondering this dilemma, Harry had a brilliant idea: he could create his own FX trading course and make money from students who would be willing to pay him to learn how to trade in the FX markets.

After all, Harry was a stockbroker and had immersed himself in the ways markets move and the tools and techniques to master these markets. He had also become a pretty good salesman as well. With some regained self-confidence, Harry began to lay out his sales pitch. This market was tailor-made for the "little guy." The new FX brokerages were making it as easy as possible to get retail customers by offering trading accounts for as little as a $500 deposit and giving their customers up to 400:1 leverage. In what other market could an investor make such huge potential gains?

But Harry knew from his brokerage background that trading in any market was very difficult—and generally not a place for amateurs. Maybe he would be doing potential traders a real service if he could teach them some techniques that would slant the odds a bit more in their favor. Sizing up where his life had gone and what had happened to his beautiful family, especially when he looked into the questioning eyes of his daughters, Harry knew he had to take the chance. FX was the only way out for him. If he could just start a school and get enough students to apply, he might make a decent living. Not great, but certainly enough to be able to get another home and live a better life.

It would certainly be better than having to live with his parents and depend on them for his family's livelihood. This had to happen, or else Jennifer would leave him for sure. Her family was appalled by what happened to their daughter and granddaughters. Although they had originally liked their son-in-law and the life he had provided for their daughter, they lost respect for him now that he had nothing. Harry had to take this chance, and he had to succeed.

SUMMARY OF CHAPTER 1

1. FX trading is in a category of its own.

Most professions and skilled trades have high barriers to entry. They generally require years of advanced education and training. In FX trading, there are not any tangible barriers to entry other than the amount of your account deposit. Nonetheless, one should not be fooled by this because successful FX trading demands several prerequisites that pave the way for profitable trading.

2. The market answers to no one.

Most traders have their own rituals or superstitions they believe can help them manipulate the market. However, at the end of the day, the market answers to no one. There is no secret tactic, no holy grail, and no magic formula. The market is a code, but any attempt to break it will prove futile. Thinking it is possible to predict and figure out the market is a delusion that most traders fall prey to.

3. It is hard not to be a follower.

Although most people understand the "herd mentality," understanding it does not make one immune to it. When the whole world seems to be going in one direction, it is nearly impossible to resist the urge to jump on the bandwagon and go along with it. This is an innate human trait, and it takes a truly headstrong individual to defy it.

4. A market-neutral approach is crucial.

Harry thought that his five years of trading experience made him a seasoned professional. However, being a pro means more than just being able to make money on the buy side in an extended bull market. Being a professional trader means being able to make money in both bull and bear markets. If your number of buy and sell trades is not approximately equal, then you are market-biased, with disaster lurking around the corner.

5. High leverage is a virtue and a vice.

With a margin account leveraged at 2:1, Harry got himself into enough trouble. A leverage of 400:1 in FX, a market tailor-made for the little guy, would present traders with even more trouble. While this high leverage is often used to lure the average person into FX trading, traders should be wary of the substantial risk attached to it.

6. The volatility of the FX market is nonpareil.

Stock market trends can last years. FX markets go through uptrends and downtrends from hour to hour and day to day. Depending on the time frame in which one trades, these markets can go from positive to negative in less than an hour. Hence, FX traders should be fully prepared for market volatility.

7. Trading is not for the emotionally volatile.

Trading is an emotional roller coaster, and it is not for everyone. It brought emotional highs and lows for Harry, from the joys of extravagance to anxiety attacks and depression. Traders who partake in FX trading need to adopt a rational perspective and prevent their emotions from misguiding them.

8. Always remember the unpredictability of the market.

Don't think you are a good trader just because you made money in a bull market. Most people will make money in such markets. It is also important to recognize that one can get carried away after a prolonged period of profitability. When this happens, most people take on more risk than they should, ultimately losing all the gains they made and more.

CHAPTER 2

HARRY DEAN'S FX TRADING SCHOOL

The year 2002 marked the beginning of Harry's foray into the FX trading world. He began to put ideas together for his FX trading school. According to Harry's business plan, he would need to attract an initial enrollment of thirty students, each paying him a $2,000 tuition fee for what would be an intensive two-day "life- and career-changing" FX-trading course. Harry's marketing plan was to follow the multilevel marketing (MLM) method made popular by companies such as Amway and Herbalife. Harry had several friends who were so-called "independent owners" in these companies, and they claimed to have had great success attracting new members using MLM sales strategies. Encouraged by their proclaimed success, Harry placed ads in his local newspapers and "penny saver" publications and put promotional flyers advertising his course in car windows. He also paid college students to hand out flyers to people on the street.

Within the first two weeks, Harry managed to sign up ten students. By offering them a cash bonus of $200 for every referral they brought in, Harry gained another twenty-five students within the following two weeks. He now had thirty-five students signed up in a little over a month. This was a marketing home run and proved that the MLM strategy worked. In his promotional materials, Harry used the following selling points:

- Tired of being a slave to a job you hate? Looking for a better way to a better life?
- Want to have the freedom to work as little or as much as you want, day after day?
- Want to work from anywhere in the world?
- What's stopping you from being successful?
- Want to learn a surefire system to make all the money you could ever want? Trade the world's largest financial market, and pull as much money as you want from it.
- Learn my insider trading secrets. My course will teach you everything you will ever need to know to make more money than you ever dreamed of.
- Change your life forever. Make money based on market volatility, regardless of market direction—up, down, or sideways.
- Enjoy taking control of your financial future, and do it from the comfort of your own home at any time, day or night. Develop a lifelong skill that will give you the life you've always dreamed of.
- Act NOW! Do it today! Sign up for my course, and change the rest of your life forever!

Harry had another brilliant marketing idea. He offered a free two-hour introductory trading course in which he demonstrated the power of his trading system. In this free course, he would pull up actual charts on a viewing screen in his classroom and show where he entered the EUR/USD pair at a high and made money by selling it short. Alternatively, he would show his students how he made money by buying and going long using his proprietary trading techniques. The intro course idea worked very well because his closing sales pitch was a discount of $500 on the full trading course if students signed up within thirty minutes of the close of the intro course. Harry had an 80 percent success rate in signing up new students from this tactic.

The major currencies and their designation in the FX market are the US dollar (USD), euro (EUR), Japanese yen (JPY), British pound (GBP), Australian dollar (AUD), Canadian dollar (CAD), and the Swiss franc (CHF). A currency pair is the quotation of the relative value of one currency unit against another currency. The quotation EUR/USD 1.2800 means that one euro is exchanged for 1.2800 US dollars.

The beauty of "hindsight bias" is you can always know the outcome, since it is based on events that have already happened. So the advantage of Harry's trading course was the fact that he (like all other FX trainers) would display a historical price chart demonstrating where he made trades by buying or selling. In reality, those supposedly profitable trades could never be validated by anyone because they never took place. Since his students did not know this, they would just nod their heads in agreement with his demonstrations because the trades Harry "took" were so obvious that anyone with common sense could see the wisdom behind them; the trading system always picked the right spots to get in and out of the market, and its results were always profitable.

In fact, the trades Harry used in his examples could not have been reasonably predicted. He was relying on the human need to find order in the world by creating memory distortions, which typically allow us to believe that such events are predictable. By presenting examples with hindsight bias, Harry made his students believe that they too could acquire superior currency trading abilities through his method. Fortunately for Harry, there was never a student in his classes brave enough or smart enough to challenge his examples.

To create an attractive image for his training classes, Harry rented a fashionable-looking computer lab located in his old brokerage firm, where a friend and former colleague was now the managing partner. Since the office was closed after 7:00 p.m. and on weekends, it made sense to make use of it during that downtime, and Harry's friend was very supportive of his trading-school idea. The two had been close while Harry worked there, and he had given his friend many hot tips that allowed him to make money during the dot-com era. Allowing use of the impressive facilities was, in part, payback for Harry's past help.

Harry's years as a stockbroker taught him that image and prestige are everything in selling, so he typically went out of his way to create an upscale image in his training establishment to impress students. This way, he could implicitly command authority and respect from his students. Harry figured that this "shock and awe" approach would lessen the likelihood that one of his students would challenge him by requesting to see his lackluster FX trading records or question the premise of his teachings. To further affirm the upscale look, Harry realized that he also had to update his wardrobe so that he looked every bit the image of a successful, wealthy trader. He did so by buying five new Brooks Brothers suits, four pairs of expensive shoes, and several shirts and ties to match. Harry was particularly conscious of his shoes, and he always kept them spit-shined to a level that would make a marine envious.

With a short, two-day training course schedule, Harry believed he could perhaps do as many as three to four weekend courses a month. Harry was counting on the fact that he would be able to bombard his students with so much trading information that they would suffer from information overload during the two-day weekend trainings. Through this tactic, Harry thought he would be far less likely to be faced with questions that might raise doubts about his credibility and reputation as an expert FX trader. His plan was to teach his students all about using multiple moving averages; Fibonacci numbers, chart patterns; Japanese candlesticks; trend lines; support and resistance levels; and indicators such as MACD, Ichimoku, fractals, Bollinger Bands, Stochastic, Commodity Channel Index (CCI), and the Relative Strength Index (RSI). He would teach them various moving average crossover trading strategies and price action trading techniques. As Harry stopped to think about it, he had enough material to teach for a whole month straight and not exhaust the information he had obtained on FX trading. This put him at ease, knowing that in the valley of the blind, the one-eyed man is king.

The sad truth is that there are hundreds of indicators available to traders and new indicators are created each day. Technical indicators are simply small components of an overall trading system and not systems in and of themselves. Indicators have many fanciful names, and they are open to intepretion and exceptions, and yet many trading books continue to popularize indicators.

What Harry did not plan to tell his students was that while all of these methods worked, they did not work consistently. They would all seem to work when the market was following a major trend by moving either up or down. Unfortunately, the markets did not always go just up or down. They also went sideways and would make zigzag patterns that could wipe out an unsuspecting trader in a matter of minutes if he did not recognize what was happening. This fact, and the fact that most new traders start trading with too small of a capital account, was the reason most FX traders ultimately blew up their trading accounts. Some would reload and plunk down more money in their trading accounts thinking, "This time, I'll get it right and make the money I've dreamed of all my life." But that rarely happened. Most often, the trader would go through yet another account, and the scene would replay itself a few more times. The markets would always win, and the battered trader would give up and never trade again.

Harry would teach his students how to recognize chart patterns, such as head and shoulder, double tops and bottoms, pennants, flagpole, and cup and holder, and demonstrate how these patterns would lead to certain results. He would reinforce this by pulling the same type of patterns from multiple FX market charts to prove his point. He would not be lying because one could empirically show that these patterns proved their validity on countless FX charts. The only thing Harry would not tell his students was that these chart patterns were no guarantee that traders would end up with the same result every time. Again, hindsight bias always worked in his favor because the market was not predictable in real-time trading.

Still, both new and experienced traders love chart patterns; it gives them a sense of security, a sense that somehow the market will obey and unfold the same way it has in the past. In fact, for every time these patterns recurred, there was a significant number of times in which they didn't. Harry knew that countless courses and trading books made huge money off of novice traders selling the same trading advice. But Harry marveled at how people never lost hope that they would find the way to get rich. There was always a fresh crop of doe-eyed wannabe traders ripe for the picking, and Harry Dean planned on picking his share.

Harry saw the value of providing his students with an overload of trading information. Then again, what he would not tell his students was that he was teaching them basic trading information that was freely available on the Internet and in books. He also would not tell them that virtually all losing traders used the same information and trading techniques to one degree or another. If these techniques really worked, wouldn't everyone in the market get rich? Well, of course not, because these techniques did not work consistently, and most would not work at all when a market was not trending, which was the majority of the time. Some of the techniques would only work enough to keep traders interested. However, they were by no means profitable over a long period of time. No matter the trading technique, and no matter what the so-called experts on TV would say, the market had a mind of its own. Only the very select few, who had many years of trading experience and who had created their own edge through dedication and research, ever made money on a consistent basis. But, of course, Harry would not tell his students that.

• • •

Jennifer watched Harry leave the house every day for his insurance company job. She knew he hated every minute of it, but he had to cope since it provided them with some money that they used to contribute to his parents' household. It allowed Jennifer to hold her head up somewhat. Obviously, the good old days were truly behind them, and she was slowly growing accustomed to her reduced circumstances. She didn't like it, but she could deal with it. She was consoled with the fact that Harry was not part of that crazy brokerage business anymore.

Reflecting back on his trading days, Harry recalled that the true edge in trading was knowing something others did not. For the majority of the time, however, he had made market decisions based on the same information others had access to. Since virtually all traders can perform common technical analyses, read the newspaper, watch the financial news, and access real-time price and news feeds, whatever information traders have access to is already reflected in current prices. In other words, the market has all the fundamental information "baked in" by the time the little retail traders actually make their trades, and this holds true for every market. This meant Harry had to come up with something that would give his students a trading edge—but what would that be?

In his brochures, Harry went to considerable lengths to describe how trading could liberate anyone from the drudgery of his or her current financial situation and the fortunes that could be made if one were serious and followed his tutelage religiously. To create that compelling edge for his trading school, he claimed to have developed a proprietary, moving-average crossover indicator on the EUR/USD currency pair. A crossover occurs when a faster moving average (shorter period moving average) crosses a slower moving average (longer period moving average). This trading system would show his students precisely when the market was going up, so they could buy and when the market was going down, so they could sell. He claimed that stocks were bad for traders because the market went up only on third of the time. The rest of the time, the market could be going down or sideways.

Harry warned them that the odds were against traders in the stock market. In FX trading, and using his proprietary trading system, his students would be able to make profits in both up and down markets. They would be able to double their chances at pulling money from the market.

As time went on, Harry refined the details in his promotional literature to make his course irresistible to potential students. He understood that all thoughts, feelings, and actions are based on survival, reproduction (sex), and social status. Harry realized that it was the emotional triggers ultimately centering on these needs that got students to sign up for his courses. Potential students didn't make decisions based on logic. Instead, decisions were made on an unconscious level and then rationalized with the conscious mind. By dangling the carrot of need, craving, and desire, he was appealing to the typical irrational human being. Students were twice as motivated to avoid pain as they were to obtain pleasure. Consequently, Harry capitalized on the fear of missing out on the opportunity of a lifetime to achieve financial freedom. By also offering limited risk and the potential for unlimited returns, Harry was able to appeal to the irrational human mind.

His revised pitch highlighted the following principles:

- A trading account can be opened for as little as $500, making the new trader's risk extremely low, but there is the potential for virtually unlimited upside when you start to make the right trades consistently.
- Making money in the FX market is not difficult. For a $2,000 investment in this course, someone can learn to trade the market for the rest of his or her life and, more importantly, learn to repeat profitable trades over and over for the rest of his or her life.

- News occurs around the world twenty-four hours a day, making the FX market extremely volatile. Learn to make money off people from their greed and fear during the volatile news releases.
- What's stopping you from being successful? Make a living by trading, and trade your way to financial freedom. It is a win-win situation.
- You don't need to guess the market. Take action! Do it today! Do it now! I promise you, I will teach you everything you need to know to make money. It is my proprietary insider strategies that will make this possible.
- Our success depends on your success. By making money, one can have the financial resources to help others.

Harry had another brilliant idea. He added a testimonials section to his sales literature where he himself wrote glowing testimonials about the genius and the effectiveness of his course. He invented five fictitious students representing various genders and nationalities—a broad spectrum of people who reported amazing gains using Harry's system. Some claimed to have doubled or tripled their trading accounts within the first month of starting to trade. The imaginary student who did the worst in the group made merely a 20 percent return during his first month of trading.

To Harry's surprise, he was now getting more and more real testimonials from his actual students. What he did not realize was that his forged testimonials had become a benchmark for his students. They would try to outdo each other to get better trading results so that they could get bragging rights and look like a star trader. Harry was thrilled with the positive feedback, but he always knew at the back of his mind that the results were not sustainable. In order to obtain those results, he was aware that students were taking excessive risks, as well as experiencing a bit of beginner's luck in an uptrending FX market. Harry was quite familiar with market uptrending. The previous uptrend in the stock market lasted nearly five years and was the major reason why he had been a successful broker.

Within six months of starting his course, Harry was pulling in over $50,000 per month. He began thinking of ways to expand his business and hiring employees. If only I had thought this up while I was in Chicago, maybe I could have saved our beautiful home, he thought. But that was water under the bridge. The future was now looking bright once more. He would have his old lifestyle back again, perhaps even better than before.

• • •

Although Harry was very happy with the success of his new trading school, he knew from his past experience that trading—be it stocks, bonds, options, commodity futures, ETFs, or FX—was very difficult and required years of training and actual trading experience before one could expect to make money on a consistent basis. Trading was not something to be ventured into with the rent money. Most of the professional traders Harry knew had blown up their accounts on numerous occasions and had to start from scratch all over again. In fact, trading was so difficult that nearly 60 percent of all the pro traders Harry knew were no longer in the business. They had opted for the steady paycheck of a job that did not depend on the day-to-day, hour-by-hour fluctuations of the market. After all, it was pretty hard to feed a family if you never knew from one week to the next if you were going to beat the market. And the real truth was that, for most traders, the market would always win.

Harry knew most Americans were nine-to-five employees working at jobs they hated. He knew that there were literally millions of unsatisfied people all over America dreaming about a better life, a life of freedom where they were their own boss and could schedule their own hours and not be accountable to anyone except themselves. They longed for a life where they could have all the money they could ever want.

What better way to advance his course sales than by offering this much-sought way out through the FX market? A market that was open five days a week, twenty-four hours a day. The hours of the London market—the world's biggest, with the most FX volume—were by far the most important and influential FX market hours. For those wanting to trade throughout the London market hours, it meant trading from 3:00 a.m. to 11:00 a.m. (eastern time). Harry did not think it necessary to tell potential students that, though the markets were open twenty-four hours a day, there were really only three hours' worth of trading if you lived on the east coast and wanted to get a normal eight hours of sleep. Those hours were from eight to eleven in the morning, eastern time—the period when the end of the London FX market trading day overlapped the first three hours of the New York FX market (the world's second largest) and consequently produced the most trading volume in the day. These were the hours when most US-based professional traders traded. The truth was, one could not trade any time or any place as advertised due to the low trading volume.

Harry's sales pitch also appealed to people's longing for freedom by stating that FX trading was so flexible that you could trade from the beach if you wanted to. Just think of it, he encouraged prospective students: sitting on the beach, watching the waves roll in while drinking a piña colada—what could be a better way of making money? In reality, none of the professionals would perform their trading at the beach since it takes immense focus to follow the market. What Harry and other FX professionals secretly knew, however, was that the extreme emotionality that grips even the most stout-hearted trader could absolutely kill that trader's good judgment and lead him to make stupid trades. For the novice trader, the emotional roller coaster could be extreme, especially if he is playing with money he really cannot afford to lose. Therefore, despite being a nice fantasy, trading on the beach remains a dream for virtually all novice traders.

In currency trading, currency pairs are traded in units of 100,000 or one standard lot size. If a trader opens a long position of one lot for the EUR/USD for the asking price of 1.3000, he is purchasing 100,000 euros while, selling 130,000 USD. An entry point is a price where a trader opens a position in the market, and an exit point is a price where he or she closes his or her position. A take-profit price is the rate where the existing position is closed out to lock in the profit, while a stop-loss price is where the existing position is closed out to limit losses.

On his website, Harry stressed the beauty of leverage as a selling point, and the leverage that FX offers traders cannot be denied. With a small $500 account, many brokerages will offer their customers a 400:1 leverage ratio. This means a trader could control $200,000, or two "standard lots," with a relatively small amount of money. However, what Harry and the brokerages knew is that most retail traders have far too little in capital in their trading accounts. A $500 account virtually guarantees that the trader will lose his or her entire trading account in an instant because there will not be enough money in the account to allow the trader to set large enough stop-loss positions; therefore, the new trader will set up his or her stops too close to his or her entry point, and, invariably, the market will move through the stop, taking out his or her position before heading back up or down the trend the trader was betting on. Once again, what in theory seems perfect usually never plays out the same way in real life. As the old saying goes, "If it sounds too good to be true, it probably is."

Harry's next selling point was that, unlike with stock or other markets, there were only four major FX pairs that the FX trader needed to consider. By far, the EUR/USD represents nearly 30 percent of all trading volume, followed by the USD/JPY for another 17 percent, the GBP/USD for 14 percent, and the USD/CHF for about 5 percent. These four major pairs accounted for more than two-thirds of the $2 trillion daily market in 2002.

Though it sounded simple, Harry knew the statistics showed that 92 percent of all FX traders lost money. These weren't very good odds, but he knew most of his students would be asking themselves why they shouldn't be among the 8 percent—after all, they could be just as successful as the professional traders, right? This was classic newbie thinking: "I can beat the odds."

• • •

Harry began spending less and less time with his family. He was gone all day at his day job, and on the weekends he would teach his courses. On the nights that he was not giving his free introductory FX classes, he went to his small home office right after supper to work on ways to enhance the marketing of his trading school. Jennifer was happy that Harry's venture seemed to be successful. She worried, however, that in his haste to regain their old lifestyle, he might not have been honest and aboveboard with his students.

The girls missed their father, as he no longer tucked them in at night. Harry had become so engrossed in his school that he hardly paid attention to them. Even though Jennifer had spoken with him about it on more than one occasion, he hadn't changed his routine to make more time for his daughters, or for her, for that matter. Their love life was suffering, and Jennifer could not remember the last time they made love. She knew that it wasn't because of another woman. Harry didn't have the time for an affair, but she still worried that she and the girls were losing their man.

SUMMARY OF CHAPTER 2

1. FX scammers know what buttons to push.

Almost everyone (except for a very few fortunate ones who have found their passion and have made it their life's work) wants to find an exit from their day job. Most people are bored and frustrated with what they do for a living and dream of a way out, a way that will provide them and their families with a secure and stable life. Fortunes are made every day by the unscrupulous who feed off this universal longing. The fact is that FX trading is a very risky venture for novice traders, and the deck is stacked against them, despite the marketing propaganda that says otherwise.

2. FX trading classes do not give you a trading edge.

All FX trading classes teach basically the same variety of indicators to their students: moving averages; candle formations; chart patterns, etc. They teach pretty much the same rudimentary trading strategies, methodologies, and theories that are widely available on Internet sites and in trading books. These courses contain virtually no unique proprietary information that can't be learned anywhere else. What the amateur trader won't be told in these courses is that whatever method or system he is being taught will not be effective on a consistent basis.

The methods taught usually work just enough to keep people interested, until frustration sets in over time, as system after system fails to live up to what its creators guaranteed.

3. The market is impossible to predict.

People tend to oversimplify the market with only three market movement conditions: uptrending, downtrending, and sideways markets. However, the market also exhibits seven other conditions: downtrend to sideways market, sideways market to downtrend, uptrend to downtrend market, downtrend to uptrend market, uptrend to sideways market, sideways to uptrend market, and consolidation. It is nearly impossible to predict which way the market will move next, given its extreme lack of uniformity.

4. Hindsight is always twenty-twenty.

In all of the trading examples that Harry shared in his classes, he had the benefit of hindsight bias, meaning that he can show where his trading system worked. He doesn't show where it did not. The unsuspecting student gets only the most positive view of Harry's trading systems. Over the long term, it is not really a trading system, and there are no fixed conditions. It is open to a lot of interpretation and is quite subjective.

5. FX traders must start trading with significant capital.

One should consider trading in the FX market only if he or she has an adequate supply of surplus capital that he or she is not worried about losing. Most informed FX traders will tell the newbie that he or she should have a minimum of $25,000 of disposable income to start trading with, and this money must be truly disposable. Most new FX traders open trading accounts with $2,000 or less, and virtually all of them lose their entire trading accounts one or more times, often causing them to quit trading after a year. The statistics show that approximately 92 percent of all traders lose money in the FX market after three years.

6. The high leverage is a slippery slope.

One of Harry's key selling points was the magic of leverage the brokerages provide to the FX trader. At a 400:1 ratio, winning trades can quickly make really good money for the trader. Leverage is a double-edged sword, however. A trader's account can be wiped out quickly by the effects of leverage. Many old-time traders will suggest that new traders not use anything above a 50:1 leverage ratio because they will be able to stay in the game longer, maybe even long enough to learn how to trade before their capital account is gutted.

7. Beware of testimonials.

Testimonials reflect a trader's experience only at a specific time or with a particular trade. However, they do not reflect the overall rate of return over a long period of time, say three to five years. And Harry's technique of fabricating his own testimonials is one of the oldest tricks in the game.

8. Everybody is using the same market "tricks."

What is your trading edge? What unique information do you think you have over other traders? Which indicators, price patterns, news feeds, price feeds, candlestick formations, trading systems, or technologies do you exclusively use? If you don't have a unique source of information that gives you an edge, you are more likely to lose all your money in FX trading.

CHAPTER 3

EVERYONE WANTS TO GET RICH

In Harry's introductory course, he demonstrated how his proprietary, expert trading techniques led to spectacular results. Being the consummate salesman he was, after two hours of demonstrations, he had twenty people register for the full two-day intensive course. What sealed the deal was his 25 percent discount for those who signed up immediately at the end of the introductory course; that amounted to $500 off the regular course price, a substantial discount to the untrained investor. Of course, this was a very common and effective high-pressure sales tactic Harry had borrowed from the infomercials he saw on television. He had always felt a pull to product pitches that offered immediate "discounts" off the full price if buyers were to "act now," and the same seemed to hold true for his students. Dangling the carrot of an immediate $500 discount was a compelling sales practice that Harry knew would work time and time again.

To stack the deck more in his favor, Harry had five paid actors, three men and two women ranging in age from twenty-four to sixty, who immediately rushed to the course registration table at the end of the introductory class. Their "enthusiasm" created a buzz among the crowd and psychologically spurred the undecided to sign up. Harry had read studies on group behavior patterns that explained how people change when they join crowds or groups. They become more gullible and impulsive and anxiously search for a group leader. They react with their emotions instead of using their intellect. People who become involved in a group become less capable of thinking for themselves and are more likely to follow others. The studies Harry read showed that intelligent people under the influence of a crowd would place more stock in the opinions of others, particularly the group leaders, than they would in their own instincts.

Many new traders tend to join chat rooms and forums looking for such group leaders. As a result, group members who follow each other in trades may catch a few trends and make some money. However, in the long run, they tend to fall prey to groupthink. Rather than critically evaluating information, members quickly form opinions to match the group consensus. This tendency is most dangerous when a respected leader influences or bullies others to share his or her opinion. Mass hysteria is a form of groupthink seen during the 1637 tulip mania (in which a single bulb sold for more than ten times the annual income of a skilled craftsman), the "dot-com" bubble of the late 1990s, and the more recent housing-market bubble, in which investors and traders got carried away with higher and higher prices. All of these cases illustrate the crowd mentality—everyone wants to be part of the action. Successful traders, on the other hand, are independent thinkers who do not have a problem being a lone wolf.

• • •

Jennifer didn't quite know what to make of Harry's newfound success. He told her all about it, but something just did not sit right with her. The money seemed to be coming too easily. Could it be possible to make this much money in such a short time and from such little work? When Jennifer would catch herself thinking that way, she'd tell herself that it was her background that caused such apprehension. She grew up in a middle-class family whose roots went back to working-class men and women who had toiled a lot harder than Harry ever did to earn a living.

There just seemed to be something wrong with making so much money so fast. Funny, she thought to herself, this had never been a problem for her while Harry was making even more money working as a stockbroker. Maybe that was because she knew that stockbrokers made lots of money. But here, Harry was doing something "off the grid," and maybe that was the reason she found it difficult to accept. He explained the various sales techniques he used to get students to sign up. The $500 discount she was okay with, but hiring actors just seemed wrong to her. Nevertheless, she kept these thoughts to herself, and the fact that the money Harry made was put into their family savings account allowed her to make peace with it.

Jennifer desperately wanted to get their own house again. She didn't know how much longer she could bear living with Harry's parents and still keep her sanity. Harry's father was great and very supportive. However, she and Harry's mother never seemed to click, and this had been true since the beginning of her relationship with Harry. Jennifer knew that as soon as they could afford a new house (and it didn't have to be grand, like the one they'd had to leave behind), she would feel much better about her mother-in-law and about herself. Her self-esteem suffered as a result of everything that had happened, and living with her in-laws only compounded that feeling. But she never confided this to Harry because she didn't want to make him feel even worse about himself and his failure in the brokerage business.

Harry's new venture with the trading school took him away at night after he worked at the insurance company all day long. Jennifer worried that he was burning himself out, and with Harry being on heavy medication in addition to the workload, she was concerned that he might collapse from exhaustion or, even worse, have a heart attack. On the contrary, Harry seemed to be flourishing. The spring was back in his step, and he seemed much more self-confident. His mood, which had been very depressed for months, was gradually coming back to its old cheerful state. He smiled more and was far more optimistic.

He was getting back to his old self in the bedroom as well. He now wanted to make love two or three times a week, whereas for months he had not wanted anything to do with her physically, which had hurt Jennifer deeply. They always had a wonderfully healthy sex life, since they first started dating and even after the kids had arrived. Jennifer took this as a source of pride, since all her other friends had told her that their sex lives with their husbands had become virtually nonexistent.

Jennifer reminisced about the first time they had made love. Harry had taken her to the best French restaurant in Chicago, where they had a meal that to this day had never been equaled. Afterward, they went to see a foreign film at one of the few art house movie theaters in town. It was a Danish film with English subtitles that centered on a love story with an abundance of graphic sex scenes. Looking back at that night, which she often did with great nostalgia, Jennifer considered it one of the most romantic and arousing evenings they ever had. After the film, Harry took her to the Four Seasons Hotel bar for a nightcap. An hour later, they had checked into a hotel suite and spent the night making wild, passionate love. Jennifer had the best sex of her life that night. She gave herself completely to Harry. She had never told him, but until that night, she was a virgin.

The next morning, after a room-service breakfast of hot chocolate and croissants, they made love again. It seemed that Harry couldn't get enough of her, nor she enough of him. She never knew that sex could be so magical and have such a profound effect on one's feelings of joy and well-being. Jennifer knew deep in her soul that Harry was her man and always would be. He was her first lover, and she couldn't see herself with anyone else, ever. When she'd mentioned this to her girlfriends, they told her she was a throwback to another era.

Now, for the first time in many months, she thought she could see some light at the end of the very long, dark, scary tunnel they were in. If only this new venture would be successful and provide the security they both yearned for. Jennifer prayed to God every day that their ordeals would be over for good. She knew her husband was a good man and a loving husband and father. She was just unsure whether his desire to provide for his family and be successful would overcome his moral values. She prayed Harry would not compromise his ethics and principles.

• • •

In one of Harry's two-day, intensive FX trading classes, a group of about ten of the students developed a friendship. One of them suggested that they set up an informal study group, just like in college. The purpose would be to share trading information using Harry's techniques, and they would meet at least once a month. They would report their successes and failures and follow trades together. Through this process, they thought they would each become better traders and make a lot of money. Within six months, three people quickly abandoned the group, as well as their trading aspirations. What had excited them and driven them to FX was eventually not able to keep them in it. The lure was fast, easy money. Why did they leave? Was it their lack of commitment and perseverance? Or was there something that they eventually recognized that made them cut their losses early and abandon this form of trading altogether?

Harry knew that not all of his students would fall for the easy-money attraction of FX trading. He knew there would be some who, after practicing his methods and trading techniques, would quickly realize that trading was hard and would take years until one was considerably proficient in it. New traders who blew up demo account after demo account—simulated money trading accounts that allow the trader to conduct fictitious trades—quickly got the picture. There is no easy money in FX trading.

The group of ten was reduced to seven and consisted of Cynthia, Charlie, Jane, Joey, Arthur, Ron, and Michelle. Cynthia was a driven real-estate investor and agent. She had done well in the real-estate market, but she wanted a way to make more money and not be dependent on the ups and downs of the real-estate business. Charlie was unemployed, having lost his job because of a personality conflict with his boss. Jane was a housewife who wanted to establish her own self-worth. Joey was a recent immigrant from Hong Kong and an avid gambler. Arthur was a software designer looking for a way out of an occupation that no longer interested him. Ron was a successful businessman looking to expand his success into other areas. He was also an adrenaline junkie with a huge ego that constantly needed new challenges to be satisfied. Michelle, the youngest of the group, was a recent college grad looking for a quick way to start earning a living and begin paying back her enormous student loans.

• • •

Cynthia's Story

Cynthia was what most people would refer to as successful. Her income was over $100,000 a year. Many would even call her wealthy with that kind of money, but success and wealth are relative. Cynthia's net income after taxes was about $65,000, and with that, she paid down a large mortgage on a comparably large house in a very nice part of suburban Chicago, an area where the real-estate taxes are high. Since she was a real-estate broker and needed to drive clients to view properties, she had bought a new Barolo red Mercedes S550 to create a prestigious image for herself.

Cynthia mingled with a group of friends and clients who loved to talk about how successful they had become by investing in real estate and the stock market. They all appeared to Cynthia to be much wealthier and more successful than she was, and this really drove her crazy because she knew that she was just as smart as any of them. She was also driven by undying ambition. Cynthia was thirty-seven, and in six months she would be thirty-eight. She had made a promise to herself to learn how to trade. She read half a dozen books on FX trading, and she became fascinated by the concept of the fight between the bull and bear for dominance of the market and how this resulted in the establishment of "support" and "resistance." After searching around for several months, she came upon Harry's trading school and attended one of his introductory two-hour courses. She was quite impressed with Harry's teachings on the inner workings of the market.

The way Harry had explained it in class was that when prices go up, bulls feel optimistic since they expect the prices to rise even higher. The bulls don't mind paying more because they want to buy high and sell at even higher prices. It is a tug of war, and the losing side is being pulled toward the torture spikes, causing it to shed tears, blood, and money. As the market continues to go up, the bears want to cut their losses. They are forced to exit their sell positions using buy trades, which pushes prices even higher. As market prices rise, it flushes out even more short positions, causing more buy trades to cover their short positions; thus, the uptrend rally feeds on itself.

When prices slide, bears feel optimistic and sell short, expecting the prices to drop even lower. The bulls' side is now being pulled toward the torture spikes and is doing its share of the bleeding. Again, the bulls want to cut their losses and must exit their buy positions by using sell trades, which pushes the market prices even lower. Falling prices flush out more long positions, who must sell to cover their trades, which further feeds the downtrend. Harry's students were impressed with his explanation of market movements but wanted to know how to apply these lessons to making money in the FX market.

To help explain, Harry would put up the chart demonstrating what happened to prices as the financial institutions stepped into the market. Using a EUR/USD chart, he showed where the support and resistance levels coincided with the Fibonacci levels of 38.2 percent, 50 percent, and 61.8 percent. He would then ask the class where they thought other individuals and institutions were placing their stop losses. Harry reminded his students that large institutions and banks play a very big role in the FX market and that they have a great incentive to push prices to the stop-loss levels of the bulls and bears. In order to make money in this market, Harry told his students, they must be in tune with the market, and they had to follow the institutional money. Unbeknown to his students, this was the standard line for all great FX storytellers. Book authors and FX lecturers commonly use the fanciful allegory of the bull and bear. Their tales are all based on hindsight, describing events that shaped market behavior after the fact. The underlying market dynamic is another matter entirely. It is extremely difficult to anticipate the market consistently, and the storytellers are unlikely to predict what is going to happen next in real-time trading. If a storyteller is consistently successful at predicting the future, he is much more likely to be trading as a full-time job and enjoying the mammoth profits from his trades.

• • •

FX trading seemed like the perfect fit for Cynthia. Harry's course was relatively inexpensive, and the potential upside was enormous. She felt that this was just what she had been looking for. If she could make trading work, she would gladly give up the cutthroat real-estate business for good.

Armed with the knowledge she had gleaned in Harry's trading course, Cynthia found herself watching the FX market at every free moment. One of the beauties of this market, she had been told, was that it was a twenty-four-hour operation, and anyone could follow it at any time of day or night. This is precisely what Cynthia did. She would stay up late at night, sometimes until two or three o'clock in the morning, to follow the "action." On nights when she went to bed before midnight, she would awake around five the next morning and continue to follow the market. Since she didn't start her real-estate job until 9:00 a.m., this left her a good three hours to watch the market and trade.

Between house showings, she would check the FX market many times a day, which allowed her to keep track of the market as it unfolded throughout the day. She opened a free demo account with a well-known FX brokerage house and began trading mini lots in the FX market where one pip equaled one dollar. In currency trading, one pip equals 1/100th of a percent, or one basis point. Cynthia found that "scalping" was the trading method she liked best, as the rush of frequent trading action got her adrenaline flowing. This method required a close watch of the market because scalping involves getting in and out of trades very quickly. Unlike trend following, the goal of scalping is to make a few pips per trade, but since more trades are made than with other methods, one could theoretically make money more quickly and with less risk of the market turning against the trade in a drastic way.

Cynthia figured that if she could make just ten pips a day, she should be able to turn a $2,000 FX account into $13,700 after three months and into $178,000 after seven months. She constructed her plan from some of the techniques Harry taught in his course and also from bits and pieces she had picked up from various forums and brokerage firm websites.

The details of Cynthia's plan were as follows: open a trading account with $2,000 in it, on which she planned to earn 5 percent (a hundred dollars) per day for the first month. Making that much money per day should be easy, she thought, as it required profiting by only ten pips each day. On average the EUR/USD currency pair moves approximately 110 pips a day. Profiting ten pips out of the daily 110 pips movement is only 9 percent of the trend. Trading ten dollars per pip, she should be able to earn a hundred dollars per day with ease. At the end of the first month, she should have $3,800 in her trading account. During the second month, she would continue to target ten pips each day. However, she planned to earn 5 percent per day of $3,800. This would require her to trade nineteen dollars per pip, which she would do by adjusting her trade size; she should be able to make $190 per day based on a gain of ten pips per day. At the end of the second month, she should have $7,220. During the third month, she would continue to target ten pips each day. She planned to earn 5 percent per day on the $7,220 balance in her account at the end of the second month. This would mean making $360 a day. Trading thirty-six dollars per pip, she figured she should be able to make $360 per day. By the end of the third month, she thought she should be able to turn her account from $2,000 into $13,718, with only eighteen days of profitable trading a month.

Cynthia was a smart person. She realized that risk and reward went hand in hand. Therefore, she considered losing trades in her plan as well. For instance, since there were twenty-two trading days for each month, she allocated two losing days, for which she would need two winning days to offset. This would yield her the eighteen days of consistent profitable trading. Cynthia was a bright student in high school and college, and her marks were always close to 100 percent. This knowledge gave her the confidence that she should not have any problem achieving 90 percent winning days out of the trading month; after all, she thought, she was certainly smarter than at least 90 percent of the other FX traders out there.

Cynthia's plan is a prototype of the typical novice trading plan. There were several major flaws in the plan. First, she assumed that she could achieve 90 percent winning trades, the same success rate she had enjoyed in school. However, in school, students are rewarded for the correct answers, and points are not taken away for the wrong answer. One's score is the cumulative total of the right answers. Trading is like the game of *Jeopardy!*, where money is awarded for the correct answer, but money is also taken away for the wrong answer. In life, no one can claim that 90 percent of their decisions are correct. Cynthia assumed a reward-to-risk ratio of 1:1 for her trades, which is extremely difficult to achieve. Assuming zero spread (the difference between the bid and ask price, also known as the spread), a win of ten pips would require a maximum loss of ten pips. But her trade would likely get stopped out before it could move in her favor. Most traders who have a high percentage of profitable trades tend to use large stop losses in order to avoid being stopped out. If the reward is ten pips and the risk is eighty pips, then the risk-to-reward ratio is 1:8. For every losing trade, Cynthia would need eight winning trades to break even, but she had accounted for only two losing days per month. This plan was overly optimistic.

Second, Cynthia did not realize that she was being fooled by the word *average* and that average is not the same thing as normal. By way of illustration, from January 1, 2000, to December

29, 2006, there were 1,824 trading days. Thirty percent of those days (543 days) had a trading range from forty to eighty pips for the EUR/USD. If Cynthia were trying to earn ten pips per day during those small-movement days, she would have needed to capture anywhere from 12 percent to 27 percent of the trend. All of a sudden her task would be three times harder than the original goal of capturing only 9 percent of the trend.

Today's world is becoming increasingly complex, and we tend to oversimplify information for ease of comprehension. The concept of averages is one of these comprehension tools, and it can be extremely misleading under certain circumstances. If we assume that stock market returns are normally distributed and form a traditional, bell-shaped curve, outliers are the two extreme negative and positive tips of this bell curve. These two extremes are not representative of the rest of the sample, so we tend to ignore them because they are unlikely to occur. A better representative of the bell curve is its average. The problem is that average is not normal, and focusing on average leads us to be blindsided when outliers occur.

In 2008, the *Wall Street Journal* covered a study that shows the significant impact that outliers have had in history. Those who conducted the study took the daily returns of the Dow from 1900 to 2008 (29,694 days) and then removed the ten best days, and the result was about 60 percent less money compared to those who remained invested the whole time. However, when the ten worst days were removed, the result was three times more money. The outliers skew the results so much that they make the average meaningless.

According to the 2010 US Census, the average number of children per family for all families was only 0.94 children. The average number of children in families with children was 1.86

children. So the next time you hear the word *average*, be wary. Isn't it terrible to consider 0.94 of a child? What part is missing?

• • •

Nobody could tell Cynthia that she couldn't consistently make ten pips a day. To her, it was sure to be child's play. In fact, she thought she should be able to do much better than this, even factoring in the broker's two-pip spread per trade. She would trade the EUR/USD exclusively, with her broker charging her a two-pip fixed spread per trade. Since she wouldn't be involved in high-volatility trades, the spread should make her broker more than happy, especially since she would be trading larger lot sizes that increased the broker's overall profit.

Cynthia's simple logic led her to believe that her broker would want to see her make as many winning trades as possible. After all, that was how brokers made money, wasn't it? With a client making more trades, the broker would be earning more profits. If the client lost at some point, he or she would no longer be a client, since his or her trading account would be gone. If a client blew up his or her account, the broker would get nothing, so it wouldn't make any sense that a broker would want the client to lose; instead, she reasoned, the broker had to be in the client's corner.

Cynthia was proud of her plan. It was based on simple mathematics, and there was no stress, no crazy, robot-trading systems, no requirement to make hundreds of pips a month to triple or quadruple her trading account. Harry's course had taught her the difference between a goal and a plan—a goal was just a desire with no action statement to achieve that desire, but a plan would help get you there. Cynthia's goal was to make $178,000 after seven months and achieve financial freedom, and her plan served as the road map.

• • •

Like many FX instructors, Harry taught his students how to create a good trading plan and execute it, increasing their chances of trading success. Harry instilled in his students that "failing to plan is planning to fail." By planning their trades, students would not trade without a stop-loss or get out of a trade too soon. A good trading plan also kept his students from just entering and exiting the market on a whim. Harry explained to his students that many traders moved from one trading technique or method to the next—not because the methods did not work, but because the traders did not apply them consistently and abide by the system's rules. Harry recited the same spiel every time:

- The fault is not with the technique, system, or method, but with the trader's failure to execute it properly.
- Traders often jump from one technique, system, or method to another before having mastered any one of them. They don't apply enough time and effort to learning. All trading systems will go through a period of drawdown. A drawdown is the peak-to-trough decline of an investment and is usually quoted in percentage between the peak and the trough. This is an unavoidable risk and must be undertaken to obtain the reward in the market. Unfortunately, humans are wired to avoid pain and to pursue pleasure and security on a golden platter. Once a

system experiences a drawdown, many traders will quickly move on to another trading system in search of one with zero risk. It is the never-ending conquest for the holy grail.
- Few traders have the patience and discipline to follow through consistently.

Harry told his students that market behavior is beyond their control. However, traders can control their ability to plan and to execute. Harry would also tell his students not to focus on the outcome of one individual trade. They should be disciplined enough to execute their trading plan and to be patient—a critical factor in successful trading. A good trading plan is useless if it is not executed properly. Most traders fail because they are constantly adjusting their strategies after a few losing trades. Hence, it is important for all the students to focus on the overall results over a large sample of trades before they change trading methods.

What Harry didn't tell his students was that a good statistical sample of trades is generally considered a minimum of one thousand trades over three to five years, with an equivalent number of buy and sell trades. There were also two critical elements that Harry failed to mention to his students when they were creating their trading plans: (1) the unknown unknowns and (2) the untested assumptions. There are known knowns, things that traders know they know. There are the known unknowns, things that traders know they do not know. But there are also unknown unknowns, things that traders do not know that they do not know. And there are a great many untested assumptions for new traders to identify, test, and challenge, such as what is the chance of a broker going bankrupt? When the *Titanic* was first designed, the assumption was that it was unsinkable. There were no prototypes to test out this assumption. Traders must challenge their trading plans and their assumptions, and doing so will allow them to stand on solid ground. Plans often fail because the assumptions have changed while the plan remains the same.

Harry did recommend that his students trade with demo accounts for at least three months before trading live with real money. When they wanted to go live with real money, he suggested that they open a "mini" account with a few hundred dollars. This prospect really excited his students because it emphasized what they considered the most attractive features of trading FX: (1) one of the lowest barriers to entry for any trading market, (2) low starting capital, and (3) only a few months of demo trading necessary to prepare a new trader for the real market.

These new traders were like sheep being led to the slaughterhouse. They had no idea they were doomed to fail due to their lack of training and practice. Harry did not tell them that trading is no different from any other field—that it takes more than ten thousand hours to become a professional. If his students were to practice trading eight hours a day for 365 days, it would take them approximately three and a half years to reach the professional level. Harry would never reveal this ugly truth because no one would ever sign up for his course if they knew it.

• • •

When his students were not profiting in their demo accounts or in live trading and asked why they were having so much trouble, Harry would always put the onus on them. Did you use a stop-loss in place? Was it too close to your entry point (trades need some room to "breathe," you know)? Did you have a planned exit strategy? Did you follow your trading plan to a T, or did you get scared and bail out of your trade too early? Were you too greedy, staying in the trade too long, even though you had hit your initial profit target? Generally, his students were guilty of committing at least one of these trading "sins," so they never considered that maybe the problem was that Harry had oversimplified trading by making it seem as if even a child could do it and make money.

Harry always had a fallback explanation that no student could refute. If his students did everything right but were still losing money, he would assert that it was the fault of their trading plans and that they should be changed. Harry always had an answer, and no one could point an accusatory finger at him for very long.

• • •

Cynthia felt great that she had a goal and a trading system that made sense to her. It was moderately easy to implement, and she believed that using this system, she would be able to make $178,000 after the first seven months of trading. Her system was fast and easy to learn and didn't require trading genius. The most important thing was that to make an easy ten pips, one only needed to conduct some technical analysis, but not very much, really. FX was not gambling; it was a serious business, which, if treated like a serious business, would generate real wealth.

Cynthia had read on several websites that 90 percent of FX traders lose money. Cynthia realized that it was not an accident that only 10 percent of FX traders actually make money. She believed that they were the ones who had done their homework and developed a system that they followed with discipline. She had begun trading in a demo account every day and at various times of the day. She knew that a live account would be different, but she also knew that the underlying principles and math of her system were sound. By using the right math, statistics, and indicators, she would trade her way to a bright new future.

The fact is that only the elite people do make money for a living trading FX. However, these people do have a gargantuan edge over all the average traders. Yet many new traders still believe that it is possible to make an easy living from FX trading. Cynthia believed with all her heart that having a good system was the key to success. She looked at her system from every angle, and she could not find one fault in it. She knew that winning at FX was not a game of chance or luck. Knowing this, she also knew that she had to be able to make money trading FX because she was just as smart, passionate, and persistent as anyone, not to mention willing to work harder than anybody on the planet. To her, success was not so much about ability as it was about attitude. She had the intelligence, personality, and ambition necessary for success.

She had read many negative posts on the various online trading forums she visited as well as from her trading circle. People would ask, “If trading is so easy, why is it so hard to make money even in a demo account?” “If making money from FX trading is so easy,” others asked, “why doesn’t everyone just quit their jobs and trade?” Some contended that many are simply unaware of the opportunity. Now that Cynthia knew about the opportunity, she felt she had been presented with a gift from the universe, and she had to seize it.

Cynthia came across a website that promoted a trading system very much like hers, in which one starts out with $1,000 and makes a 25 percent profit each month. In two years, the 25 percent profit would compound to more than $210,000. This example reinforced Cynthia's belief in her system, and it made her very happy to see that there were other people in the trading community who believed in a similar type of system.

She was grateful to the members of her trading circle who had been so supportive, as well as those in the trading forums who believed like she did. She had made a commitment to herself and to her trading friends to follow through with her system and to practice, practice, practice until she achieved the results she knew she could achieve. She was also very thankful for Harry's trading course, which had opened up this new world of FX trading for her. Without Harry's course, she knew she wouldn't have known where to begin.

Cynthia believed that FX was a business, and in business, nothing is impossible when it makes logical sense. In the beginning, she would concentrate on trading only one pair. She thought that the best pair to concentrate on was the EUR/USD, the currency pair with the largest daily trading volume and little likelihood of market manipulation. A few institutions simply can't control enough volume to be able to manipulate this pair effectively, she thought. Also, because the pair was so commonly traded, she felt she could get good spreads from the brokers, which would reduce her trading costs.

Cynthia would use only one account to trade this pair. That way, she wouldn't be distracted, which seemed to happen to so many people she chatted with on the forums. They simply got distracted by trying to follow too many pairs and indicators at the same time. She would keep her focus simple and pure. She would also watch the financial news and read the trading sites to see the reactions to market activity and help her plan her trades.

She would also use the chart indicators that she liked best in planning her trades. These were the exponential moving averages, the Relative Strength Index, Stochastics, chart patterns, and candlestick formations. From what she learned in Harry's trading course, this should be enough to get her going. All of this information was enough to follow for one pair; she didn't know how people could use multiple indicators and follow multiple pairs. She guessed it must come with experience. Perhaps one day she would follow multiple pairs, but for right now, she would be smart and stick with just one, the big one, the EUR/USD.

• • •

After trading in her demo account and following her trading system during all of her free time, Cynthia came to the conclusion that one could conceivably make ten pips a day because the EUR/USD moved that much every day. She found herself easily making ten pips a day in her demo account. After demo trading for two weeks, Cynthia was convinced that her system worked. It was so clear to her that she couldn't understand why more people were not enjoying the same success.

Ten pips a day was easy to make, she thought. This was not magic or wishful thinking. This was putting a well-thought-out and mathematically proven method in place and seeing it work. It was like the science classes she took in university where they had lab sessions, and she had to conduct experiments. She started out with a theory and then applied it to the real world to see if it held up.

Trading was empirically credible, but it required education and on-the-job experience to become successful at it. Cynthia closely compared learning FX trading to receiving her university education. One definitely needed to become educated in the discipline, which is why she spent so much time watching the charts and the fundamental and technical analyses she found on various FX websites. She reasoned that if she wanted to become a successful trader, it was very much like becoming a doctor, lawyer, or rocket scientist. The ones who were persistent and diligent in their studies would be successful, but there was no escaping the need for lessons and homework.

Cynthia came to believe that people who were unsuccessful at trading FX either didn't really have the necessary desire, or they were just not willing to put in the time it took to get educated. She thought that FX trading attracted many who were just in it for a quick buck. Since the barriers to entry were so low to open a trading account and start trading, and in light of the great sales pitches given by the various FX brokerage houses, many people saw winning at FX as their road to the easy life. Almost all of these people would lose the entire contents of their accounts very quickly. Some would put more money in, only to lose it all again, and on and on it went. These folks did not have the desire, the system, or the education needed to make their FX trading work. She would not be like them. She would succeed.

Cynthia believed that to be successful at FX, one had to have a strong desire and interest in trading itself. It couldn't just be about making money—if that was the only motivation, one would probably not make money. For Cynthia, FX trading had become a passion. She loved the way her expertise was growing day by day and how she was able to select the right entry and exit points in her trades. She felt she was surely getting the hang of it.

• • •

With ten pips a day and focusing on a 5 percent return each day, Cynthia had fallen into the "compounding" trap. Albert Einstein is attributed with the statement, "Compounding interest is the greatest mathematical discovery of all time." Einstein died in 1955, yet the first mention of this quote in association with the genius was more than twenty-five years after his death, so it is unlikely that he ever uttered the words. It is more likely a case of name dropping in the financial industry. It is to the industry's advantage to impress potential investors by linking the famous physicist with the concept of compounding. Nevertheless, the magic of compounding (sometimes called compound interest) transforms investment money into a powerful income-generating tool. Compounding is the process of generating earnings on assets' reinvested earnings. To work, it requires two things: (1) the reinvestment of earnings and (2) time. The more time you give your investment using compounding, the larger it will grow.

Originally, compounding was used in yearly interest calculations for bonds, but it has been used more recently as a sales tool to fool new FX traders. What Cynthia did not realize was that a 5 percent return each day on her trading account was the equivalent of a 90 percent return per month. The ten pips a day fallacy originated around 2000, shortly after the FX market was deregulated and the small retail investor was allowed to play with the "big boys" in the FX market. Its sole purpose was to help promote FX trading to the small retail trader. If someone were able to obtain a 90 percent return each month starting with a $2,000 account, that person would be able to generate more than $4.4 million after twelve months due to the magic of compounding. Since the opening of the FX market to retail investors, there have been no verifiable trading results of anyone achieving such a return. Yet, the ten pips a day compounding fallacy prevails as a selling point for all manner of FX systems, courses, and brokerage accounts.

The notion that it is possible to make ten pips a day consistently is a fallacy. It is nothing more than a slick marketing device that FX scammers love to use on the unsuspecting newbie because it seems so logical and easy to understand. After all, math doesn't lie. This sales trick sells hope to people who want to get rich quick, but the devil is in the details, as the following conditions are required: (1) capturing the right market movement each day, (2) being 90 percent successful with all your trades, (3) compounding the return to 90 percent each month, (4) having the patience and discipline to execute each trade according to your trading plan, and (5) somehow accelerating the normal learning process so that it doesn't take ten thousand hours of study and practice to become proficient at trading.

Being able to earn ten pips a day and a 5 percent daily return on one's trading account would be like generating a million dollars by asking a million people for a dollar each. The math works, but the logistics makes it highly improbable.

SUMMARY OF CHAPTER 3

1. Beware of "groupthink" in trading.

A person who becomes involved in a group becomes less capable of thinking for himself and is more likely to follow others. Mass hysteria is a form of groupthink. Traders should always learn to question conventional wisdom and not associate popularity with effectiveness.

2. Be aware of high-pressure selling tactics.

Scammers love to offer an immediate discount to force buyers to act swiftly on fear of missing out. Nothing is going to change one's life instantaneously; hence, take a step back with a deep breath to think it over.

3. Institutions and banks play a very big role in the FX market.

These firms spend hundreds of millions developing trading models and executing algorithms. Each firm has its own proprietary methods to hide its orders and its intentions about the market so that other competing firms will not put the firm out of business. It is a myth that one can stay in tune with the market and follow the institutional money.

4. Traders must always challenge their trading plans.

All FX trainers urge traders to create a trading plan and to execute it with discipline. However, this tactic does not guarantee success. There are also unknown unknowns and a great deal of untested assumptions within the plan that new traders must identify, test, and challenge. Challenging one's trading plans allows a trader to stand upon more solid ground.

5. The word *average* is loosely used.

Today's world is becoming increasingly complex, and we tend to oversimplify information for ease of comprehension. The concept of averages is one example of oversimplification that can be extremely misleading in some circumstances. With average numbers come outliers, which distort one's calculations.

6. Understand the positive and negative uses of compounding.

Compounding is a mathematical principle that creates large asset appreciation over an extended period of time. It is the reinvestment of earnings on invested principal over a time frame of years. Unfortunately, this principle is touted in the FX industry to entice the get-rich-quick crowd. Compounding return is then promoted over a period of months instead of years.

7. Trading is a skill that takes time to master.

Trading for a few months in a demo account represents just the tip of the iceberg. It takes years to make consistently profitable FX trades. It has been estimated that to become proficient at any profession, it takes a minimum of ten thousand hours, or three and a half years. To think that one can become a successful trader in only a few months is a total scam, a scam that is perpetrated by the industry in an effort to attract new accounts. Trading is like any other profession—it takes years of study and practice to become good enough to earn a living from it.

8. There should be no daily quota for pips.

The idea that it is easy to consistently make ten pips a day is a fallacy. It is nothing more than a slick marketing device that FX scammers love to use on the unsuspecting newbie because it seems so logical.

CHAPTER 4

INFORMATION, DISINFORMATION, AND MISINFORMATION

Jane's Story

Jane was one of the "gang of seven" students from Harry's course and was just as avid a trader as her classmate Cynthia. In fact, since she was a housewife, she could actually spend more time on her trading work than Cynthia, who had to maintain her real-estate business concurrently. Like Cynthia, Jane, too, had been searching for a way to become financially independent and prove to herself that she was much more than a housewife.

In reality, many women would have gladly changed places with Jane, for she was married to a wealthy businessman who owned seven Lexus franchise dealerships in Wisconsin and Illinois. In fact, his annual income was well over $2.3 million, and he had bought Jane a beautiful home on a ten-acre lot in one of the most exclusive suburbs of Chicago. The only dark cloud over their otherwise perfect life was that Jane and her husband had been trying for a baby for three years, with no success. Jane had had two miscarriages, and the doctors were not very optimistic that she would carry a child to term. Still, the couple wanted a child, and they were not ready to give up trying just yet, though both had discussed the possibility of adoption if they couldn't have their own baby within the next two years.

This almost perfect slice of domestic tranquility wasn't enough for Jane. She had always been a go-getter and had graduated in the top 2 percent of her class at the University of Wisconsin. She majored in finance, which she loved, and thought about continuing on to get her PhD so that she could teach at the college level. However, when her husband, Peter, began to court her ten years ago, he was so full of confidence that she was swept up in his dream of becoming a successful businessman. Jane did what so many other women had done in the past and basically subordinated her life to her husband's. After graduation, she and Peter, who had a brand-new MBA, got married with the blessings of both of their families. Shortly afterward, they set up a house in a nice, but definitely not ostentatious, two-bedroom house in the Chicago area.

Peter had started out as a salesman at a local Mercedes dealership and did extraordinarily well. He found he had a gift for sales and business management. One day, a customer made him a business proposition that he couldn't refuse—he would finance the purchase of the only Lexus dealership in the Chicago area if Peter would run it for him. Not only would Peter be paid a very generous salary for running the dealership, but he would be given an 18 percent ownership stake as well. Needless to say, Peter accepted the offer and never looked back. Peter made his first million dollars at the end of his first year running the Lexus dealership, and his income continued to grow every year thereafter. He couldn't believe his good fortune—he had found a business that made him an excellent income and for which he seemed to have a natural ability.

Despite their good fortune, Jane was not happy. They had no children, and although they had started going to a fertility specialist, the future seemed grim. On the face of it, she had everything most women would want: a magnificent home, household help, and a wealthy husband who truly loved her. Despite all that, she felt empty. The lack of children was certainly a factor, but it could not fully explain the general sense of dissatisfaction she had. This feeling evolved into longing for some sort of life of her own, something outside of her day-to-day existence that would provide her with a sense of accomplishment and satisfaction. Accordingly, she began to look around for opportunities to make her own money.

For Jane, making her own money was always a way of validating her own self-worth and independence. Even as a young child, she would try to get her parents to pay her for doing chores around the house. When she was in high school, she always had a job after school and on the weekends working at the local mall. She didn't even really need to work since her parents were very comfortable, but Jane needed to make money to prove to herself that she was a valuable and capable human being. Why she had this drive, she did not know. Perhaps it had something to do with the fact that she suffered from a mild form of Asperger's syndrome. Diagnosed when she was just six, Jane had difficulty with her social interactions in school. She was somewhat withdrawn, and her speech patterns were unusual, which caused most of the other children to shun her. She did have one good friend, a very shy girl who was also excluded by the other children. They became inseparable. As Jane grew older, her Asperger's seemed to become less and less of an impediment. Though she still did not mix easily with others, it was certainly much less uncomfortable than it had been for her when she was younger.

On the plus side of the equation, when Jane was interested in something, it became an all-consuming passion for her. Her mild Asperger's gave her what people called "tunnel vision," in that she would place all her attention into a very narrow area and seemingly consume everything there was to know about that subject. This had been a big help to her in school, and as a result, she was always at the top of her class. Her parents had been very concerned about their daughter, and they sought out the best medical and psychological help they could find in the state. They had been told by experts that Jane's degree of Asperger's was not severe, but it would always be with her to some degree or another, not necessarily in a negative way. In Jane's case, it was certainly a positive to be able to concentrate on subjects of interest to an extreme degree.

Jane was walking downtown one day when she was handed a flyer promoting Harry Dean's FX Trading School. Instead of just throwing away the flyer, as she would have done 99 percent of the time, she hung onto it. For some strange reason something about the flyer had caught her attention, and she wanted to give it a closer inspection when she got home. That evening, Jane looked over the flyer, and something about FX trading struck a chord in her. With a desire to learn more, she attended one of Harry's free two-hour seminars. This is perfect, she thought. She ended up signing up for the two-day course that same night.

Harry's course made her light up like a Roman candle, and she was smitten—hook, line, and sinker, she was a believer. Even more than Cynthia, Jane not only saw learning how to trade FX as a means to prove that she was her own person and could make her own money, but she also saw in the FX market a creature of compelling beauty. The markets and their price action charts were splendorous things to Jane. Like pieces of priceless modern art, each chart seemed to have its own character and unique way of expression. To Jane, it was like watching a drama unfold; the fact that one could make money from trying to predict the direction of the market seemed wholly secondary. She had fallen in love with this mysterious and beautiful thing called FX.

She told Peter about her interest in learning FX trading and her plan to take Harry's course. Peter didn't know anything about FX, but he could see that his wife had latched onto something that brought a new joy to her life. He was a smart man and knew that if his wife was happy, she would make his life happier as well, so he supported her new "hobby."

For her part, Jane became a fanatical student of the FX markets and trading systems. She experimented with numerous other systems on top of several trading systems Harry had demonstrated in class. She finally settled on using a combination of trend lines, the weighted moving average of five and twenty crossovers, and the Fibonacci retracement and extension. She was not a fan of indicators or candlestick patterns. Jane believed that trendline drawing was the most reliable method, and everything else was secondary. She developed her very own system based on five different techniques to draw her trend lines. On any given chart, it would take her thirty minutes to draw the trend lines five different ways. She would draw and redraw multiple times before she was happy with the outcome. She would then put different emphasis on each trend line via color and thickness. She never deleted her thickest trend lines since she found that they could disappear off a chart and then come back two or three months later. Jane felt that most traders didn't spend enough time on trend lines because they were too busy focusing on their indicators. She limited herself to trading only the EUR/USD pair and its six time-frame charts: the daily, four-hour, hourly, thirty minutes, fifteen minutes, and three minutes. Jane disagreed with various FX trading forums because she found that there were too many self-proclaimed trading gurus on them giving out misleading trading advice to newbies. Successful traders, she thought, were lone wolves and independent thinkers and researchers. She could not comprehend how people traded based on a single time-frame chart, whether it was a four-hour or daily chart.

She also felt that new traders didn't realize that they could never be successful trading multiple-currency pairs. They had to learn to specialize and see the interaction of multiple time-frame charts and trend lines on a single-currency pair. She thought that when trading one currency pair, traders had to look at six time-frame charts. Therefore, to properly trade ten different currency pairs, they would have to look at sixty charts. Many traders took shortcuts by focusing on a single time-frame chart so that they could trade multiple currency pairs instead of being limited to one. Their justification was that there were more opportunities to profit with multiple-currency pairs. Jane believed that to develop an edge in trading, one must specialize instead of being a generalist. After all, if you had a heart problem and required a bypass, you would trust a cardiac surgeon to operate on you much more than your family doctor.

Jane was spending more and more time on her trading. She knew her Asperger's was in large part responsible for her manic focus on her trading, but she didn't care. It is true that some people are born with a gift that gives them a big step up in the world of investing. Warren Buffet, for instance, was a child prodigy who became interested in the stock market when he was only nine years old. He was also born with a photographic memory. For him, the stock market became an all-consuming passion at a very early age, and this eventually led him to become one of the wealthiest men in the world.

People like Jane with Asperger's syndrome and other forms of autism also seem to do well in trading. Experts believe that this is due to their amazing ability to concentrate and focus on a very specific area. They are then able to see things that "normal" people can't. There are many nongenius types who do very well trading FX and other markets. However, these people have trained themselves to concentrate and focus on their trading over five to ten years of study and practice. This character advantage in most cases comes from many years of hard work rather than innate qualities.

Jane's mild form of Asperger's created a trading edge for her, similar to Warren Buffett's photographic memory for reading financial statements. Unfortunately, most trading newbies are not born with an edge and, consequently, are handicapped when competing with people such as Jane or Warren Buffett. In the FX market, traders are competing with the best and brightest minds in the world, and yet many FX educators still promote the idea that FX trading is for everyone. Traders are doomed to fail unless they are fortunate enough to come across someone or something else to provide them with a trading edge.

Jane was getting profound satisfaction from her new hobby and was spending seventy to eighty hours a week on it. She would even draw and redraw her trend lines and analyze her charts when the market was closed on the weekends. Peter was away tending to his business most of the time, and the housekeeping was done by the maids she had hired several years back. Since they did all the cleaning, laundry, and cooking, Jane had very little else to do anyway.

Jane couldn't understand how anyone could believe some of the ridiculous FX marketing hype she had read on the various forums and even by authors of published books. Some claimed that one needed to trade only five hours a week to achieve success in FX. What a scam, she thought.

Jane would spend two to three hours just analyzing a potential trade before she would decide whether to take it. She would not take a trade unless she felt it would generate at least a 2:1 reward-to-risk ratio, regardless of whether her target was twenty, forty, or a hundred pips. She saw a trade as a general would view a battle: every conceivable contingency was planned for before she pulled the trigger and made a trade. And all this time she was still trading a demo account, with no real money at risk. She couldn't imagine that she would be more dedicated once she actually started real trading with real money.

Several months passed, and Peter was becoming uneasy about the growing distance he felt between Jane and himself. At first, he was glad she had found a hobby, and he knew all about her Asperger's and understood the extreme focus someone with the disorder could become locked into. He was not sure they were at a point yet where Jane's trading was a really serious problem. After all, she was just "play" trading. She wasn't risking real money yet, and it was keeping her busy. Peter decided to hold his tongue a while longer to see if she would calm down and lose interest in this new pastime. He decided to give it a few more months.

But Jane realized that she was actually becoming a pretty darn good trader, and her winning trade percentage was 65 percent and growing. She suspected that her Asperger's syndrome helped her gain an edge in trading as it had in school. Her ability to concentrate was far superior to other people's, allowing her to spend long hours every day planning her trades. She would calculate and document her entry and exit points on multiple time-frame charts that she was trading in. She would take multiple screen captures of the different time frames based on her decisions on entry and exit points. On top of that, she also recorded her emotional states—her highs and lows as the trades progressed. After each trade, she would write a post-trade analysis in her trading journal, and she kept track of why she made every trade and how each turned out. Unlike thousands of other traders, she was not focusing on or anticipating the outcome of each trade, since the market took its own course. It was not about the profitable or losing trades. She was more interested in the process that led her to enter and exit each trade. She understood that she was responsible for her trades. However, she could not control the results, even when she executed everything perfectly. She knew that there was an element of randomness to the market. Hence, it was crucial for her to maintain at least a 2:1 reward-to-risk ratio for long-term sustainability. She would review all the trades she had made during the week and would sometimes go back several months further. From this record keeping, she had a trading log that yielded invaluable information to her. Constantly reviewing her trading log showed her, in the clearest detail, what worked and what didn't. Jane was becoming a successful and proficient trader, and while she absolutely loved this, she loved the process that led her to become successful just as much. For Jane, the journey was as much fun as the summit.

• • •

Joey's Story

Joey was another a member of the gang of seven from Harry's trading school. Unlike the others, Joey came from a much different background. He had immigrated to the United States some five years earlier when his family, who had lived in Hong Kong, decided that they preferred living free from Communist rule. Joey was a very lucky man, as his family had considerable wealth from its export business, which they still ran through surrogates in Hong Kong while living in Kenosha, Wisconsin. They moved to Kenosha because they had other family members there who had left Hong Kong just prior to the 1997 handover of the region to the Chinese by the British. Joey was fifty years old and married, with three teenaged children.

He had been very good at the family business and helped it grow into a multimillion-dollar enterprise. Unfortunately, Joey had a love affair with gambling. He had picked up the habit years earlier while on a trip to Macau with his uncles, all of them inveterate gamblers. There was something about all of the blinking lights and the fast action that got his heart pumping like nothing else. He was infatuated from his first foray into a casino. With Macau just a quick ferry ride from Hong Kong, Joey found himself going there every weekend, even though his wife gave him substantial grief about it. After a while, his wife gave up and let him go without complaining—after all, he was a good provider.

His betting record was mixed, and although he lost somewhat more than he won, he didn't let himself lose more than the amount he had set aside as his "play money." In many ways, Joey loved the atmosphere of action that permeated the Macau air as much as the gambling itself. Macau was a magical place for Joey. He also liked the easy access to female companionship that Macau offered. In addition to all this, the food and accommodations were excellent and reasonably priced. Considering all Macau had to offer, Joey couldn't think of any place he'd rather be on the weekends.

Everything changed when he and his family moved to Kenosha. It was not his idea—in fact, he had voted against it, but he was outvoted by the family elders, and in Asia, family duty always comes first. Joey's comprehension of written English was quite good, but his speaking was dreadful. He knew that his kids would get a better education in the United States than in Hong Kong, and, more importantly, they would be Americans and would fully integrate into American society. It was important for his children to have their father around while they were growing up. They moved to Kenosha when they were very young, so they grew up speaking English as well as the Cantonese that the family spoke at home. They even spoke very good Mandarin as well, thanks to their grandparents, who were fluent in that language. A bright future was sure to be theirs—with so much business being done with China these days, and with a shortage of Mandarin speakers in America, his kids would likely find good jobs.

Nevertheless, Joey felt like a fish out of water in his adopted country. Kenosha, as nice as it was, was no Hong Kong. Joey felt like a total outsider even after more than five years in the States, especially since his English was only passable. The family business in Hong Kong still produced income for the family, but because he no longer needed to spend as much time on it, he found himself with way too much free time on his hands. Even though Kenosha was somewhat cosmopolitan because of the university there, Joey felt he stood out like a sore thumb.

Not only that, but gambling was illegal in Kenosha, except for the Potawatomi Indian Nation casino, which had only bingo, slot machines, and some poker. This was the closest casino around and paled dreadfully in comparison to the Macau Venetian, Sands, or the Wynn casino-hotel complexes and other mega casinos in Macau that fed the insatiable Chinese appetite for gambling. It was like a fall from grace.

Joey did not have any friends. He was homesick and felt out of place. He felt a paralyzing void that made every day a chore. He began to spend more and more time at the Potawatomi casino, even though it offered very little compared to the Macau casinos. He was now spending nearly four days a week there. He did not gamble all the time—often he just went there to see the blinking lights on the "one-armed bandits" and soak in the atmosphere. Subconsciously, he was trying to regain some semblance of his Macau experience, and even though the Potawatomi casino didn't even come close, it was still better than nothing.

Spending so much time at the casino had become a big concern to his wife and teenage daughters, and they expressed their fear that he was becoming nothing more than a degenerate gambler. Echoing those feelings were his parents; his brothers and sisters; and his many aunts, uncles, and cousins living nearby. The Chinese, being very family-oriented, are very close-knit—some, like Joey, would say way too close. They were forever getting into one another's personal lives. All of them told him he was spending far too much time gambling, and some even said that he had a gambling problem and should go to the Gamblers Anonymous twelve-step program. Joey knew they would never be able to understand the thrill he got from being in a casino around all the action and the electricity in the air. But, after months of relentless pressure from his family, he decreased his visits to the casino and was now only going once a week. Even the small comfort he had gotten from a poor excuse for a casino was taken away from him.

Gambling had been Joey's release, and without it, he felt suffocated. When he had his life centered on a single thing that gave it meaning, he risked a complete crash once it was taken away. He already felt isolated because his English deterred him from socializing, and now, with mounting pressures from his family, Joey felt like he was drowning. He could not help but wonder why life was worth living if it brought only pain on a daily basis. He found himself on the dreaded slippery slope, seriously looking at death as a release. Although thoughts of suicide had always crept in, this time he actually considered them. Joey lost hope that his life would get any better, and he began to have more thoughts of suicide. There were times when Joey wanted to put a gun to his head and end his miserable life.

Joey was eating lunch in Chicago one day. Someone had left a copy of the local Penny Saver publication on his table, and having nothing better to do, he started perusing it. While browsing through it, he came across one of Harry's FX course advertisements. As with Jane, something about Harry's ad struck a nerve in Joey. He didn't know too much about FX, other than the fact that a cousin of his had lost quite a bit of money trading the currency market. Joey had never looked into it because he always had other ways of gambling his money away, but looking the ad over, he saw that perhaps trading wasn't exactly the same thing as gambling. Maybe there was a skill someone could learn to give him or her an edge to make some good money. If nothing else, FX trading might be a new hobby to cheer up his otherwise dull and dreary life.

Like the others in the gang of seven, Joey attended one of Harry's introductory seminars, and he was immediately attracted to the adrenaline rush of FX trading. He found that following price action on FX charts gave him feelings very similar to those he would experience when he was gambling in the casino. Even though he wasn't actually trading yet, he could sense the rush it might provide. Joey signed up at the end of the seminar after Harry's "minimal risk and unlimited potential gain" pitch. He now had a new game of chance, but the great thing about this one was that his family wouldn't look at it as gambling. Trading would be considered a business. He was certain that this would mean he would get much less grief from his family. Trading FX would also provide him with more respect from the others, as it had an aura of sophistication and intellectual challenge.

Thus, Joey took Harry's two-day course. He was thrilled by the opportunity for another life that trading offered. It was similar to the games of chance he knew and loved, but it was much more respectable and would not lead to trouble with his family. In fact, if he turned out to be successful, they would admire him greatly, as the Chinese venerated money making.

Joey studied hard, spending ten to twelve hours a day, five days a week practicing various trading systems and techniques that he had learned in Harry's course and others that he had found on the many FX trading forums that proliferated on the Internet. One thing that Joey became aware of rather quickly was that many of the forums, especially the ones sponsored by the FX brokerage houses, put out very misleading information, information that would actually lead to substantial losses if put into effect by an inexperienced trader. There were lots of FX books in the libraries and bookstores, written by many self-proclaimed expert traders, but Joey's business experience had taught him that there was information, misinformation, and disinformation out there. Misinformation was false information that was spread unintentionally, especially by authors in FX trading books and traders on the forums. Disinformation was intentionally inaccurate information that was spread deliberately. Given the abundance of information on the Internet forums, libraries, and bookstores, new traders would have a difficult time discerning the truth. Unlike professional and scholarly peer reviews of an author's book in other technical fields, which typically improve the quality and uphold the standards of an author's work, in the FX world, anyone can publish trading books or create a website or an online forum, claiming to be an expert in FX trading.

Joey's research confirmed what he had thought about the availability of all this "free" trading advice that was everywhere he looked. Most of it wasn't worth a thing. He suspected much of it was disinformation given to make new traders lose their money. Coming from an Asian culture where information is kept secret and considered a source of power to be guarded, Joey viewed the openness of Western culture and its access to information of all kinds with deep suspicion. In ancient China, those who knew how to read could only be of the upper classes, and then they were allowed to read only approved writings. Indeed, it was well known at one time that if any unauthorized person read *The Art of War* by Sun Tzu or any of the other military classics, he or she and the person's families would be put to death immediately. Military books were considered dangerous knowledge, which was accessible to only a select few. This cultural belief persisted in present-day China to one degree or another. Therefore, Joey assumed most of the FX information on the Internet was really disinformation put out for someone's gain (most likely the brokerages, trading instructors, and service providers) at the expense of those relying on it. Such a free exchange of information would never happen in Asia.

Other bad information he found on the Internet was simply the prattle of foolish and ignorant amateur traders who knew nothing but thought they were trading experts. Joey saw that a new trader had to be very careful about what he took as advice from Internet sources, be they brokerage-related or otherwise. The FX trading world was just as full of nonsense as any other, perhaps even more so since there was little in the way of regulatory oversight of this market. To Joey, it seemed to be like the Wild West in the cowboy and Indian movies he had seen when he was a kid in Hong Kong. But even this aspect of FX trading had a perverse sort of appeal to him; it added to the fun of trying to overcome the odds that were obviously stacked in favor of the market and the brokerage houses, which was just like the gambling casinos he loved so dearly.

Unlike Jane, however, Joey did not have the laser-like ability to focus on one area. His ability to calculate odds was better than most, but nowhere near Jane's. Nevertheless, Joey opened a demo trading account with a brokerage firm that he had selected primarily because of the layout of its trading dashboard. It had all sorts of blinking squares on it, which showed the ever-changing prices for all the FX currency pairs being traded in the FX market. The blinking squares and the constant flashing of up and down arrows immediately took Joey back to his beloved Macau, and every time he opened his online trading platform, those memories came back to him. It was instant relief and comfort from his otherwise dreary life. It was like being able to face a one-armed bandit every time he chose to open his computer.

Joey was not as good a record keeper as Jane, either. Although Harry had told all of his students about the importance of keeping a good trading log so they could see over time what worked and what did not in their trading strategies, very few of Harry's students actually took the time to create logs, much less refer back to them for guidance on what they might be doing wrong or how they might trade better. Joey kept a log, but it had neither the level of detail nor the screen captures of his actual trades that Jane's log had. As a result, Joey didn't find logging as useful as Harry had said it would be, and after four months of half-hearted effort to log his trades, Joey eventually stopped altogether. Still, Joey's trading method—an amalgamation of Ichimoku, fractals, relative strength index, and stochastic indicators on the one-hour and four-hour charts—was giving him some success, certainly enough for him to be encouraged to continue his trading venture.

After five months of demo trading and fine-tuning his trading system, Joey opened a live account with $26,000. Why that number? Because two plus six equals eight, which is an auspicious number for Asians. In his first two months, he made $45,000 and was a true believer in the ability to make money from the FX market. He was now spending ten hours a day following the markets and managing his trades. Just like Jane, he had become obsessed with FX. He absolutely loved it. In many respects, he found that FX was even more fun than casino gambling, particularly since he could do it from anywhere using his laptop. Joey was smart enough to make his addiction look like a respectable business by setting up an office in his home, which he used only for his trading business. His family owned a small office building in downtown Kenosa where they oversaw the family's Hong Kong business and the local businesses they had acquired since moving there, but Joey didn't want to mix the family business with his trading. His family was too nosy and would be all up in his face about his trading. The less they knew about it, the better, except for the fact that he was making money from it. This will shut them up, he thought.

The months passed, and at the end of Joey's first year of trading, he had made over $250,000. He was absolutely amazed and convinced that FX trading was the best way to make a living that man had ever invented. He told his family about his success, and their response rather shocked him. Instead of being in awe of his trading prowess, they actually thought that he was merely gambling again, but in a different way. Coming from the ancient Chinese culture, doing something useful was revered. In the old times in China, there were four categories of people, and their hierarchy was scholars, farmers, craftsmen, and then merchants, also known as traders. The farmers were held in much higher social esteem than the trader class that controlled more wealth than the farmers. This respect was based on the social utility of the farmers' activity. Farmers produced food, which sustained life. Traders merely made money off of the hard labor of those that made things that were needed to support life. In ancient China, the trader class, though wealthy, was looked down upon as they didn't produce any tangible goods, only profit from others' creations. Traders were labeled as greedy and lacking moral character. Money was, after all, an intangible idea, even if represented by paper or metal coins; it was not something you could eat or use to build a house. As the trader families got wealthier, they hired scholars to tutor their sons, and many families produced scholarly officials. The traders also associated themselves with other scholarly officials through facilitation and speculation on vital public infrastructure, such as building roads and bridges. The traders also invested in budding industries, such as bookmaking. Soon the trader class gained the prestige and acceptance from the scholarly elite. Even though all this happened more than 2,500 years ago and halfway around the world, it is still true today, as money can easily elevate one's social status and respect in society.

Joey just couldn't seem to please his family. Although he still helped run the family businesses, he made a very un-Chinese decision to go against his family's wishes and continue with his successful trading career. After all, what did they know about it, and how could they judge him? How could they say that there was not any socially redeeming future to FX trading? They were just unsophisticated immigrants who were stuck in the old ways. This was twenty-first-century America, not first-century China. Traders are speculators, Joey conceded, and many are motivated by gambling and greed, but traders provide additional liquidity that enhances the efficiency of the market and are an integral part of the free-market system. Speculators reduce the cost of government capital to fund massive infrastructure projects, such as subway, bridges, the Internet, etc. The speculator, like any investor, is looking for a return on investment and is willing to take some risk. The speculator increases the chances that prices are fair by creating an environment where hedging becomes feasible. For instance, when a harvest is too small to satisfy consumption needs, speculators come in and raise the price with scarcity buying. The producer, encouraged by the high price, grows or imports more. When the price is higher than normal, speculators sell to reduce prices. This encourages consumption and exports. The producers can hedge their harvest profits by going to the market with delivery contracts. These contracts reduce the producers' risk in an event of drought, bad weather, or volatile prices.

In the stock, bond, and options markets, the markets provide a place for companies to raise capital, so they can start and run their businesses. Without capital, no business can come into being or survive for long. There are both benefits and potential costs to having speculators in the market. Suppose the market has very few speculators or a few extremely large speculators. They could create a negative situation by colluding with one another, or the few extremely large speculators by themselves could drive the price either too low or too high. In most situations, the presence of the speculators contributes to fair pricing, but at the same time, they can significantly distort prices in the market. The FX market allows governments and large financial institutions to hedge their currency holdings to reduce risk. Without the FX markets, today's global economy would be much smaller, which would mean a much-reduced standard of living for everyone on the planet. People who trade the FX market are, in fact, facilitating the smooth functioning of the world's currency markets, which makes international trade possible.

Joey's family did not think very highly of his success. Even though most of them would be considered part of the trader class, the family embraced old ways, and their ideas were firmly planted. They urged him to get into a real business, one that produced something tangible, not just money, a business that had some socially redeeming feature. Merely making money was not in itself noble in the Chinese value system. Making money while doing something that was beneficial to society was the Chinese ideal. To the Chinese, being a teacher or a physician was meaningful, but there was nothing meaningful about being an FX trader. As they saw it, the FX trader was trying to steal money from the market without being caught. The money in the market belonged to the entities that put it there. When the FX trader got caught, he would face the equivalent of having his hand chopped off by the market.

Despite his family's disapproval, Joey wanted to continue trading, and so he did. He still devoted ten hours to his system every trading day and was never far from his laptop. His family had said their piece and would not say anything more about his trading. This provided him with some relief. Joey began to sign up for more FX trading courses to further enhance his knowledge about trading. He started to add MACD, Fibonacci levels, and Bollinger Bands to his already complex amalgamation of Ichimoku, fractals, relative strength index, and stochastic indicators on the one-hour and four-hour charts. Joey believed that in order to improve his winning percentage, he must continuously refine his trading system. By adding more indicators, he hoped to filter out the losing trades and quadruple his profit.

Generally, he would exit all his trades at the end of the New York daily trading session at 5:00 p.m. New York time. So he would start everyday "flat," or with no open trades in his account the next day. He would then get up at five every morning to catch the London session activity and then would wait until the opening of the New York session at eight. He preferred to trade the 9:00 a.m. to noon segment of the New York market, as he would catch the overlap of the last three hours of the London session with the first three hours of the New York session. This was when most of the daily FX trading volume occurred. Price volatility was at its highest during this time period, and one could stand to make the most money by trading then.

At the end of his thirteenth month of live trading, Joey's trading results began to deteriorate. Instead of consistently making money, he saw his trading account lose money more often than not. At first, it started out slowly, so he took it in stride as just normal market activity. Professional traders all know that they have to "pay the market back" from time to time. The gods of the market demanded their pound of flesh. However, when every month became a losing month for Joey, no matter what he tried to do, he began to despair. How could his winning trading system fail him so completely? Within three months, Joey had not only lost the $250,000 he was up at the end of his first year, but he was in the hole by another $75,000. It had been twelve months of hard work, yet it took only three months to wipe out everything. All the traders in the gang of seven criticized Joey for his greed and claimed that they would have stopped trading when the account slid from $250,000 to $126,000. This way, he could still claim that he earned a nice $100,000 in the past fifteen months. However, they all missed the crucial point that reward is proportional to risk. Imagine a blackjack player betting fifty dollars and winning fifty dollars from the house. The same player could have bet $50,000 and won $50,000 from the same winning hand. All the surrounding observers would be applauding if a player won $50,000 from the house. However, most observers would look with disgust on a player who just lost $50,000 on a single hand of blackjack.

While he was winning, the gang of seven applauded Joey for turning $26,000 into $250,000, a whopping 861 percent return within twelve months. In order for Joey to generate such massive returns, he had to take excessive risks. His bets paid off because, by some random chance, the market cooperated. His fellow traders should have criticized him then because his gains were excessive. It seemed to Joey that there was a double standard; he was applauded for unlimited gain, but tarred and feathered for excessive losses.

Joey had to take money from his private savings (the savings account his wife knew nothing about) to continue trading. If his wife ever found out how much money he had lost, she would be furious, but the gambler in him thought that maybe the gods would smile on him once more.

• • •

Charlie's Story

Another member of the gang of seven, Charlie, was in between jobs. Charlie had been working as an IT technician in a small biotech company in Chicago, which he really didn't care for, but in light of the slow economy and the need to support himself, he stuck it out. The company he worked for really wasn't the problem for Charlie; it was his boss. Charlie had one of those bosses so many people find themselves with from time to time. He was egotistical, inconsiderate, and rude to his underlings. He had absolutely no problem demeaning a subordinate in the presence of someone else and would accept neither criticism nor constructive feedback. He would never admit when he was wrong. This was in complete contrast to Charlie, who was one of the kindest, meekest men one could ever meet.

Charlie hated going to work in the morning and actually got a knot in his stomach as soon as he entered his office. What incensed Charlie was the fact that his boss was making $250,000 a year while Charlie worked twice as hard and made only $40,000. But what Charlie failed to take into account was that his boss was also a 50 percent owner of the company, which he had built with his partner nine years ago from the basement of his house and had over $3 million at risk. Charlie was too naïve about business to understand that the rewards went to those who took risks. Charlie really hadn't put any money at risk, nor had he gone through the pain and suffering of starting a company. His salary merely reflected the market rate for his services, not an investor's return on investment or the sweat equity of his boss. Like most employees, Charlie felt entitled to more based on his fifty-hour work week.

All his boss did during the day was call in subordinates and lambast them for no reason (other than to keep them on their toes) then go out to lunch for three hours, where he would proceed to drink his meal. He would then come back to the office either all fired up, in which case all his subordinates would receive his tyrannical wrath for no specific reason, or (best-case scenario) he would fall asleep at his desk until 5:00 p.m., when he would get up and go home.

Charlie was a good worker, but the market for his specialty was very small, and there was nothing else available in Chicago that fit his skills. He was willing to move for a job, even if it meant moving to Timbuktu, just as long as it was away from his boss. But despite constant searching, he could not find any openings. The economy had put on a hiring freeze everywhere in the country. Charlie did not give up looking, however.

Charlie was in his office on a Tuesday browsing a job site when his boss barged in unexpectedly. He took one look at the website Charlie was browsing and quickly surmised that Charlie was job hunting. This outraged him, and he told Charlie to pack up his things because he was fired. As in most of the United States, Illinois is an "at-will employment" state, which means that, unless an employer fires someone for something that is considered discriminatory under federal or state antidiscrimination laws, an employer can terminate any employee's employment at will, which essentially means for no reason. Since Charlie did not fall under any of the protected categories of these laws, he had no recourse against his boss or the company. The best revenge he could hope to get was forty weeks of unemployment, but that didn't cover his living expenses; it would barely cover his food and utility bills.

Fortunately, Charlie was a frugal soul and had saved a great deal over the years since he graduated from college and started working. He had nearly $100,000 in the bank, so he would be all right for a year or so until he found another job. Being single with no children also helped a great deal. He had only himself to worry about, and he lived on the upper level of a two-family house that he owned. The rent from his tenants in the lower level of the house paid for Charlie's housing costs, so his only real expenses were his car, food, and clothing—and now, of course, health insurance, since he was no longer covered by his employer's policy.

The firing was traumatic for Charlie. He had always been the kind of person who did the right thing. Even when he was a kid, his parents never had to worry about him; he just always did what was expected of him. He never got into trouble of any kind. He didn't have any real vices, didn't drink (not for religious or other reasons, simply because he didn't like the taste), do drugs, or gamble. He didn't have a very active social life, and the last time he had been on a date was over two years ago, and that had been with a girl who was, at the time, the receptionist at his company. She had since moved on. He still wondered how he had ever gotten up the nerve to ask her out. He had no real friends to speak of, and his entire family was in Davenport, Iowa, where he was born and raised. The only reason he was in Chicago was because he had obtained his degree in information technology from the Triton College and had grown to love Chicago during his college years.

Charlie's main form of entertainment was watching movies that he either rented every week from the local video store or downloaded off the Internet. Movies were the ultimate escape from his drab and lonely life. For a couple of hours, he could forget his miserable excuse for a life and be someone or somewhere else. Now that he was out of a job but had enough money to live on for a good while, he was not so disposed to jump back into another job where he might have to work for a boss. His thoughts turned to starting his own business, where he would report only to himself. With that mind that he came across one of Harry's flyers being handed out by a cute, blonde co-ed on Main Street. Normally, he would have thrown the flyer out or just never accepted it in the first place. He decided to give it a glance this time as he made his way over to a nearby café that he frequented for lunch. Once in the café, he got a chance to thoroughly review Harry's ad, which was actually pretty convincing. One of the things Charlie noticed at first glance was the statement, "With FX trading you can become your own boss." That rang more than a few bells with Charlie, and since the flyer touted a free seminar, Charlie said to himself, What the heck do I have to lose? He attended the very next one. Charlie heard everything he wanted to hear at the seminar from Harry, and he immediately signed up for the two-day trading course.

With all the newfound time on his hands, Charlie initially spent the better part of his days reading online FX forums and trading in several demo accounts he had set up with a couple of the larger retail FX brokerages. He tried every technique and trading system that Harry had introduced to his students and finally settled on one that used the four-hour chart trading eight different currency pairs. Charlie took a slightly different track than his classmates because he was spending only two hours looking at the charts and two hours a day perusing the forums and other websites for ideas. His system used a variation of the Multiple Moving Averages (MMA) method in conjunction with the CCI indicator. When he saw that the MMAs were compressing into each other, and that the slower averages were intersecting with the faster ones, he knew that there was a trend change about to take place. Using the CCI indicator as a confirmation, he would place his trade accordingly. Since the four-hour chart did not move much, Charlie did not have to constantly monitor the market. After one and a half months of strong gains in his demo account, Charlie decided to open a live account with $2,000.

On a normal day, Charlie would spend about four hours a day on his trading activities. With plenty of free time left in the day, Charlie started watching more movies and daytime soap operas. He could not believe what he had been missing out on with all the different TV shows. Charlie also started cooking as a hobby and was becoming quite the foodie.

Charlie was beginning to realize that being self-employed was the greatest freedom in the world. It afforded him the liberty to stay up late watching movies and wake up at any time of the day. There was no need to be at work at a certain time. He didn't have to worry about traffic to get to work on time or what he was going to wear that day. Between trading sessions, he would go to the park, swim, or head to the billiard parlor. Charlie was simply spending lots of time doing all the things he enjoyed. All of the independence, control, and freedom from routine that Harry promised his students if they became successful traders were being realized in Charlie's life. Charlie's days were his own. He didn't have to report to anyone other than himself. He had never known anything like this before, and it struck him that everyone else he knew had to go to a job and work for someone else—they were nothing more than slaves, and he was free.

By the end of his first month, Charlie had turned his $2,000 into $30,000, and he was absolutely ecstatic. He had finally found the answer to his prayers. Never again would he have to put up with an idiotic boss. Never again would he be made to feel small, as he felt at his old job. At this rate, within a few years, he would be wealthy enough to buy his old boss's company and fire him.

Charlie approached the FX market somewhat differently than his other trading friends. He would first start out with a small trade to feel out the market. He would then add additional trades in the same direction. He did this out of the belief that it did not increase his original risk because the first position was smaller, and he made additional trades only if each previous trade was profitable. Using the new equity his earlier winning trades made him, Charlie would increase his lot sizes. He could do this during any of his trades by merely taking more trades in the same direction. "Pyramiding," as this technique was called, seemed to work like a charm for Charlie during a trending market.

Quickly, Charlie gained respect from the gang of seven for earning the most money during the shortest period of time: a 1,400 percent gain in thirty days. Was such respect warranted? For some reason, no respect is given to a person who spends five dollars on a lottery ticket in the morning and wins a jackpot of $12 million by the evening. This person is merely considered lucky. However, much respect is given to traders who can turn $26,000 into $250,000 within one year or $2,000 into $30,000 in thirty days. Charlie got more respect because he made a string of correct decisions during the thirty-day period to amass such gains. He must have had an edge that allowed him to make this string of correct decisions. What Charlie didn't realize was that his experience was just a statistic in a big scheme of statistical probability.

Statistical probability comes in many forms. For instance, given a room with twenty-three people in it, there is a 50 percent probability that two people will have the same birthday, excluding those born on February 29. If you add seven more people to this room, the probability goes up to 70 percent. There are 365 days in a year, excluding leap years, and we need to have only fifty people in a room to have a 97 percent chance of two people having the same birthday. Most people can't seem to comprehend that there is a 99 percent probability of two people having the same birthday if we add seven more people to the room of fifty. This is known as the "birthday paradox" probability. The FX market that is promoted to the average person is based on the most favorable probability scenarios, and, unfortunately, most people don't understand the concept of probability and how the probabilities of FX trading are stacked against them. This means that they are doomed to fail at some point, if they trade long enough.

Charlie's massive gain is a "tail end" statistic in a normal statistical distribution curve. Imagine putting one thousand speculators in a large gymnasium and asking them to predict the outcome of several coin tosses. Each speculator will decide heads or tails, and those who guess correctly will remain standing. Those who get it incorrect will sit down. After the first toss, we have eliminated half of the speculators, assuming that approximately 50 percent picked heads, while the rest picked tails. After four tosses, only sixty people are standing, and after eight tosses, there are only four people left standing. Do these people possess precognition, telepathy, psychokinetic abilities, or some other edge over the others because they are able to predict eight consecutive coin tosses? No, it has nothing to do with their decisions, but it has everything to do with statistical probability. In Charlie's case, within a short trading duration, he had, in effect, become a lottery winner.

SUMMARY OF CHAPTER 4

1. Some people are born with a trading edge.

It is true that there are some people who are born with some gift that gives them a big step up in the world of investing. Warren Buffet was born with a photographic memory. People like Jane, who have Asperger's syndrome and other forms of autism, also seem to do well in trading. Experts believe that this is due to their amazing ability to concentrate and maintain focus on a very narrow area.

2. Successful traders keep excellent records.

To be a successful FX trader requires not only extensive study, practice, and planning, but also good documentation and record keeping. All trades must be well planned out in advance, with entries and exits well thought out and firmly fixed. Details such as screen captures from before and after each trade and notes regarding one's emotional state over the course of a trade can be revelatory. In order to improve in trading, the tedious and arduous process of detailed record keeping is essential. Without a log, a trader will never learn the vital trading lessons needed to become a successful FX trader.

3. Your computer can become a "one-armed bandit."

Before computers and the Internet, you had to drive to a casino, but now the personal computer offers a gambling outlet within the comfort of your own home. Very much like an electronic game of chance, the trading platform has all sorts of blinking squares and a constant flashing of up and down arrows with the ever-changing price of all the FX currency pairs.

4. There is an abundance of information, misinformation, and disinformation available to new traders.

Given the abundance of information freely available from different sources, new traders can have a difficult time discerning the truth. The information overload clouds any sort of good judgment.

5. There are both benefits and costs associated with having speculators in the marketplace.

The FX market allows governments and large financial institutions to hedge their currency holdings to reduce risk. Without the FX markets, today's global economy would be much smaller, and this would mean a much reduced standard of living for everyone on the planet. If the market had very few speculators or a few extremely large speculators, they could collude with each other, or the few extremely large speculators by themselves could drive prices either too low or too high. In most situations, the presence of the speculators contributes to fair pricing, but they can also distort prices in the market significantly.

6. **Traders get applauded for unlimited gain but tarred and feathered for excessive losses.**

Reward is proportional to risk, so in order to generate massive returns, one must take excessive risks. Traders enjoying excessive gains are also taking extreme risks. It is only a matter of time before the risks will undo all the gains.

7. **Most traders don't understand statistical probability.**

FX is being promoted to the average person under the most favorable of probability scenarios. Unfortunately, most people don't understand the concept of probability and how the probabilities of FX trading are stacked against them. This means that they are doomed to fail at some point if they trade long enough.

8. **Traders are comparable to lottery winners.**

For some reason, no respect is given to a person who spends five dollars in the morning and wins a jackpot of $12 million by the evening. However, respect is given to traders who can turn $26,000 into $250,000 within one year or $2,000 into $30,000 in thirty days. During a short trading duration, traders can be, in effect, lottery winners.

CHAPTER 5

REAL SKIN IN THE GAME

Ron's Story

Ron was a successful forty-five-year-old businessman living in the Chicago area. He became a self-made multimillionaire by buying a run-down, old McDonald's franchise in one of the worst parts of town. He had always wanted to own a business, and at the age of twenty-five, he came across this franchise opportunity while reading the local newspaper. Having majored in business in college, Ron thought this prospect seemed tailor-made for him. With the money he had saved and with help from his father, he bought the business. He then took the course given by the McDonald's Corporation's Hamburger University, a course recommended for every owner/operator and manager of a McDonald's franchise, and there he learned all aspects of running a McDonald's and proved to be an excellent student.

His first franchise was sold at a "fire sale" price. Ron later discovered the reason for the discounted price—it was completely dilapidated. Ron had to invest twice the amount of the original purchase price to upgrade the building and the equipment. Fortunately, he had a local bank that believed in him and the McDonald's business model, and he got a loan for the necessary improvements. All told, the upgrades took about eighteen months. When the building was finally renovated, his restaurant was a thing of beauty. It was the newest and cleanest McDonald's in the area, and it attracted three times the business of the old restaurant.

Ron wasn't satisfied with owning just one McDonald's. He now knew what it took to run a successful franchise, and he found another one that was also pretty run-down. He snapped it up on the cheap and once again got the loan he needed to bring the establishment up to the highest standards of the McDonald's chain. As with his first restaurant, the families came in droves, attracted to the clean, warm atmosphere and the new décor. The food was far better than what the old McDonald's had produced because Ron had outfitted the kitchen with all the newest equipment. He used only the best-quality food available and replaced the cooking oil before it got burned, and his french fries were considered the best in the city. Word spread, and Ron's second store was doing twice the business of his first store, which itself had tripled the business of the original.

Within nine years, Ron had purchased a total of five McDonald's in the greater Chicago area and was scouting out other franchise opportunities in nearby cities. He stuck only to the business he knew—the McDonald's fast-food business. He had friends who made a lot of money in one business only to lose it all by getting involved in other business ventures they knew nothing about. Ron told himself he would never do that. He stuck strictly with the McDonald's business model that he knew inside and out. His father had always told him to "stick with what you know, and that will bring you success." His father was right.

By the end of his twentieth year in the business, Ron owned twelve McDonald's restaurants in three cities. All of them made huge profits for him. He had a corporate staff of his own to which he delegated most of the day-to-day responsibilities required to oversee operations. He had weekly meetings to go over store operations and to solve problems, but, all in all, his stores ran like a Swiss watch. Ron had a gift for spotting talent for his company. He had a sense of who to hire as his managers and how to manage them to get optimum results. He was also a tremendously charismatic guy, and everyone liked him. He never browbeat an employee; he always treated each employee, from the lowliest counterman to his regional managers, with the respect he himself would want to be shown. This was another life message his father, a devout Christian, had raised him with. Practice the Golden Rule in all of your affairs, and God will bless you, he believed, and Ron did unto others as he would have them do unto him.

There was just one problem: with his corporation established and running pretty much by itself, Ron found himself becoming increasingly bored. He was making nearly $17.8 million a year in after-tax profit. He had a beautiful 20,000-square-foot mansion in the best suburb of Chicago, a 5,000-acre working ranch in Montana, and a magnificent ski house in Aspen. He was in great health and married to one of the most beautiful women in the entire state. In fact, his wife, Darlene, in her younger years had been a Miss Illinois beauty queen and competed in the Miss America pageant in Atlantic City, where she took fourth place.

Although she wanted children, Darlene honored Ron's wishes not to have any. He didn't want kids because he felt they would take his attention away from running his hamburger empire, and to an extent, that was true. He did give generously to many local children's charities, however, including the Boys & Girls Clubs of America, the Boy Scouts of America, and several foster homes that took care of indigent children. His charitable gifts and a scholarship program he had set up managed to get many disadvantaged youths on the right track, and some of them, after finishing their schooling, ended up working in Ron's business. In fact, five were well on their way to becoming regional managers.

But Ron couldn't ignore the fact that he was jaded. He had conquered all that he had set out to accomplish. He had been a middle-class kid from a good Christian family who made good. The boredom was starting to trouble him, though, and he found himself doing stupid and reckless things. Although he didn't have a lot of male friends, he did have several buddies whom he went out with. Many nights they ended up at clubs where they drank perhaps a bit too much.

One night, after leaving a posh club with a buddy, Ron took a friend's dare and began tailgating a local police car. The game was that you had to get as close as possible to the police car's bumper without touching it and do this for thirteen blocks, all without getting arrested. As Ron stepped on the gas pedal of his Porsche 911 Carrera and revved the engine, he began to feel the adrenaline pumping through his veins. His heart beat faster as he gripped his fingers tightly around the steering wheel. His eyes narrowed to focus on the license plate of the police car in front of him. Ron increased the pressure on the gas pedal, and the needle on the tachometer began to climb. He depressed the clutch with his left foot and changed gears with his right hand, and the German-engineered machine started to growl.

Ron started to second-guess his decision to accept his friend's bet, but there was no time for turning back as the Porsche started to creep closer and closer to the bumper of the police car. Ron glanced at the blue lights of his speedometer as the needle started inching past sixty. His friend in the passenger seat had become frantic and pleaded for him to stop. Ron was on an adrenaline high now—part of him wanted to stop, but he wanted to see how far and close he could tailgate the police car. The pleading from his friend became more resolute, and the sweat began rolling down Ron's forehead. Suddenly, the lights of the cop car started to flash, and the siren started blaring. Ron's heart seemed to stop beating for the longest second of his life. He knew that he had pushed the limit of his adventure a bit too far and began mentally rehearsing what he was going to say to the police officer as he slowed down his car. Lucky for Ron, the police car started to speed up and zoomed away. Ron breathed a sigh of relief for dodging the bullet, but he couldn't help enjoying the adrenaline rush from the adventure.

All the fun from this incident did not distract Ron from taking it as a warning. He needed to find some interest or other occupation to keep his mind busy, or he knew he would end up a drunk, in jail, or both. Success can sometimes lead to ruin, and Ron was beginning to realize this. He needed a challenge, something to ignite and maintain his interest. Darlene sensed the restlessness in him and knew he was bored. Try as she might, she couldn't seem to get him interested in the things her friends' husbands enjoyed. For instance, she and Ron were members in the best country club in the Chicago area, but Ron hated golf and thought it was a complete waste of time. Chasing a little white ball around a golf course seemed the height of stupidity to him. Similarly, he considered tennis to be a girl's game and wouldn't be caught dead on the court. He did go to the club from time to time, to keep Darlene happy mostly, and having a meal at the club restaurant was nice.

While he was walking to one of his restaurants in downtown Chicago, his eye caught a very pretty girl handing out flyers. Her beauty got his attention, and the cad in him took one of her flyers just as a way to make some contact with her. She was very charming and knew how to handle herself with men and sent him nicely on his way, letting him think that he made an impression on her. As he got to the end of the block, he took a look at the flyer. It was one of Harry's FX trading course flyers. Trading? He had never even thought about it. All his money was handled by his financial manager, who had put him in a multitude of investments that optimally diversified his portfolio. Ron was his finance guy's biggest client, so he got extra-special treatment. Ron had little contact with his investments other than to review his monthly statements, which showed that his return barely exceeded the rate of inflation due to the diversification and the conservative nature of the investments in his portfolio. His financial manager believed that as long as he did not lose client funds, he stood to pocket handsomely from the 2 percent yearly management fee. He was unwilling to take any risk since it could cause him to lose clients.

Ron always had a desire to learn more about the financial world and secretly envied the "finance guys," as he referred to them. They all seemed to him to be much smarter than he was, but maybe it was just that they spoke in financial jargon that he barely understood. They, however, seemed to regard him highly. He supposed it was because he had built an actual business and made it into a very profitable empire. The one thing he knew they respected above all else was the almighty dollar, and Ron could sure make a lot of those.

Ron walked into one of his McDonald's location for an inspection, something he did frequently on an unannounced basis, and sat down in the back office for a few minutes to give the flyer a better look. What he read in Harry's flyer engaged him immediately. Here was a financial investing opportunity that he could do on his own without the assistance of one of his finance guys. This was a completely new world that he knew nothing about, but it appeared to be very profitable and didn't require an MBA. Nevertheless, it wasn't the money to be made that appealed to him. It was the challenge of conquering a new frontier, one that would certainly give him added respect with the finance pros he admired. He was hooked and went to the free seminar Harry was giving, which just happened to be the next evening. Ron found himself in the boardroom of a well-known brokerage firm in downtown Chicago with twenty other people who looked like they came from pretty much every walk of life. Harry, as always, was right on cue, and because he had been polishing his seminar material and his delivery over the months, he gave an outstanding presentation. At the end of it, he had a 90 percent sign-up rate for his two-day course. Ron was one of the first in line to enroll; he was that impressed. Why hadn't he heard about this before? He saw the profit potential immediately and couldn't wait to take the course. Could it really be this easy to make money in the FX markets?

Ron loved Harry's course and took to its concepts right away. He was eager to start trading and opened a demo account the same night he finished the course. The first three days of his demo trading had been winners for him, and he thought that trading was the easiest way to make money. But on day four, he lost nearly all of his demo account in two impulsive trades that he had taken with the increased leverage from his previous days' winnings. Ron took these trades without any stop loss because of his need for action. He didn't wait for the right setup to form before jumping into the market. Everything in his business career reinforced his attitude that he was very rarely wrong about any decision he made, and he thought this would carry over into his fledgling trading career.

Unfortunately, trading is not for everyone. This is especially true for those personalities that have a hot temper, are impulsive, or have the need to see quick action. Constantly monitoring the price chart is like watching paint dry for some people. You can change your habits, but you cannot change your personality. Knowing what type of personality you have is critical to becoming a successful trader. If you can't overcome your negative personality traits, it is best not to trade at all.

Two months passed, and Ron was still not making money in his demo account. This was shaping up to be a real challenge for him. He began reading the various online FX trading forums to see if he could find a better trading system than the moving average crossover system variation he had gotten from Harry's course. It had to be that the system was bad. If he found the right one, he would be okay. Ron found and tried six more trading systems, but none of them worked for him. Then he read a comment on one of the forums that said demo trading was nonsense; it was only when a trader put real money at risk that his attention would be sufficiently focused to make good trading decisions. In other words, he had to have real "skin in the game" if he were to be a successful trader.

The next day Ron opened a trading account with a deposit of $100,000. That, he thought, would be real enough. Within three months, he had lost the entire amount. He couldn't understand what he was doing wrong, and, for Ron, failure was not an option. He thought that maybe he needed to take more courses, and that would get him over his trading problem. This led him to take ten more intensive courses, some online, some locally, and several courses in New York. Still, he just could not become a consistently successful trader. Ron had become addicted to the market and was not learning from his mistakes.

Ron's edge over other traders was that he had lots of money, which allowed him to take many more courses on trading, system development, and psychology. What Ron did not realize, however, was that these multiday, intensive courses are filled with an overabundance of information. Even though Ron was able to pick up several useful tips at these events, he was unable to put them into practice. In order for the information to become useful and habit forming, it takes time. An example of proper training is the Dale Carnegie courses in effective speaking and human relations. The program was founded in 1912 based on its founder's teachings. More than eight million people have completed these programs, and they are conducted in more than eighty countries. Warren Buffett claimed that the program changed his life. It is the only diploma in his office, not his master's degree in economics from Columbia. In 1945, the Dale Carnegie was for fourteen weeks with one four-hour session each week. The courses were set up for students to learn over a certain period of time so that the brain can absorb and retain the new and useful information. By having the program extended over ninety-eight days, new habits are formed and reinforced until they become unconscious competence. Regrettably, by the 2000s, the Dale Carnegie course had been reduced down to eight weeks, with three-and-a-half-hour sessions each week. Too many multiday trading courses out there promise life-changing experiences. However, people tend to go right back to their bad trading habits after the several days of intensive training.

According to the *European Journal of Social Psychology*, on average it takes sixty-six days to create a new habit. However, it can take anywhere from eighteen to 254 days if the task requires dedication. In Ron's case, his need for action prevented him from being able to wait for the right setup to form before jumping into the market. It would take a lot of time and dedication for Ron to cure this habit. Unfortunately, this was only one of his dozens of bad trading habits. Like Ron, most traders need many months to rid themselves of their multiple bad habits, as it is rare that a new trader has just one bad habit to overcome.

• • •

Arthur's Story

Arthur was a thirty-six-year-old software designer and worked for a company that produced facial-recognition software. Although he loved his work, he felt that he wasn't making enough money. He was married, and his wife was expecting their first child, which only increased his money anxiety. Several of the men he worked with had made small fortunes during the tech boom of the late 1990s by investing in start-up dot-com companies, and he couldn't help but envy them. They worked for his company because they were fascinated with developing three-dimensional facial-recognition software, not so much because they needed the money, like he did. He had been too young to get in on the bubble, as he was still in school getting his master's degree in programming from the University of Wisconsin. By the time he graduated, the bubble had already burst.

Twenty years ago, facial recognition relied on two-dimensional imaging, and the subject had to be looking directly at or at least thirty-five degrees toward the camera. Any variance of light or facial expression of the subject would create inaccuracy when compared to an image from a database. The company where Arthur worked captured three-dimensional images of a person in real time. It then used depth and axis of measurement for alignment, which was not affected by lighting. The new three-dimensional facial recognition could be used in darkness and had the potential to recognize up to a ninety-degree angle to the camera. This was nearly a threefold improvement in accuracy over the old method. His company and a few others were racing to perfect this new technology, which had huge market potential.

Arthur had a friend who had just finished taking Harry's trading course and was very high on it. He told Arthur about all the positive features of trading FX, like how you could start with a small trading account and trade on your free time. His friend had also described the learning technique to trade via demo accounts; that way a newbie could trade without risking any money at all. Then, once his trading skills produced consistently winning trades, he could open a live account with real money so the risk factor was very small. Arthur's friend had known him for years; they had gone to college and graduated together, so Arthur placed great credence in his friend's advice.

Consequently, Arthur attended Harry's free seminar, just as the other gang of seven members had. He was very impressed with the profit potential that Harry demonstrated during the seminar. This could be just what he was looking for to supplement his income and—who knew?—maybe even provide him with a full-time opportunity if he learned how to trade well. Arthur began to fantasize about the lifestyle he, his wife, and their soon-to-be-born child could have if he could truly make money from this FX trading business. They would be able to buy the house they always wanted, get new cars, and provide for their new baby the way they wanted to—the best schools, summer camps, extracurricular activities, trips to Europe, and on and on his thoughts took him. Harry had sold him. Now he just had to convince his wife to allow him to use $2,000 of their meager savings to pay for the tuition to Harry's course.

Although he was convinced, he now had to make the sale with the wife, which would be easier said than done. But Arthur was a scientist and knew how to put forward an argument and defend it with facts. He took Harry's sales materials for the trading course and added his own twist to them. He then found a quiet time one evening to explain the whole thing to his wife and give the reasons why he thought spending their hard-earned money would be well worth it to the family in the long run. She was skeptical at first and, being an intelligent, young woman, asked Arthur why, if trading FX was so profitable and seemingly easy, more people didn't quit their day jobs and just trade full time. After all, according to what Harry told his classes, it was just a question of learning the right system and applying some trading rules consistently. So how come every one didn't do it? she wondered. It was a good question, and Arthur had his answers prepared. First, the market had not been available to the small, retail investors prior to deregulation a few years ago. This was the opportunity of a lifetime since not everyone was aware of it yet. Second, the reason not everyone was successful at trading was because they let their emotions get in the way of strictly following the trading rules. As soon as people got their emotions involved in a trade, they would be sure to make the wrong decisions, and this inevitably led to bad trades.

Arthur told his wife that with his background as a systems designer and programmer, he was certain that once he had learned the basics about trading and had studied and applied a number of trading systems on a demo account, he would be able to design an automated trading system that would take the emotional, human element out of trading. This would lead to a much higher level of trading success—he was sure of it. Arthur explained to his wife that trading was more than 90 percent discipline and that nothing is more disciplined than computerized trading. His wife knew that her husband was a brilliant software programmer and had taken top honors in all of his studies. She also knew he had the brains to make this work. Although not totally enthusiastic, she gave him her consent to use the family savings to enroll in Harry's course.

And so Arthur enrolled in Harry's course and proved himself to be a quick study. After the course was over, Arthur joined the other gang of seven members for coffee and agreed to keep in touch. He would manually try out all of the systems the other members were using to see which ones would work for him. Something about Japanese candlestick patterns appealed to Arthur. It was based on the legendary story of Munehisa, who amassed a huge fortune trading in the rice market during the 1700s. Some claimed that Munehisa had executed over a hundred consecutive winning trades. Others asserted that Munehisa fabricated this claim. Unfortunately, there were no verifiable trading records. Arthur went back to his wife and begged her for another $1,500 so that he could take a class specifically on Japanese candlestick charting techniques. He told his wife that if there were high-reliability bullish and bearish reversal patterns in candlestick techniques, he should be able to program them. After all, his company created 3-D software, and candlestick patterns were 2-D. It should be a lot easier to implement because the level of difficulty was child's play compared to what he was developing at work. Reluctantly, his wife agreed.

Candlesticks are graphical representations of price movement for a given period of time. They are formed by the opening, high, low, and closing prices, and there are predefined rules to match the patterns. Similar to indicators, they have fanciful names and work only some of the time. Unfortunately, most novice traders are spending lots of resources and time learning about trading tools that work only intermittently.

After the candlestick course, Arthur began to program the highly reliable bullish reversal patterns such as "abandoned baby," "morning doji star," "three inside up," "three outside up," "three white soldiers," and "concealing baby swallow." He found that none of them were consistent in predicting market reversals. Quickly, he'd bang out the code for the bearish reversal patterns like the evening star, evening doji star, three black crows, three inside down, and three outside down. Again, Arthur was disheartened and frustrated. He knew that his codes were correct, as he could manually verify each trading signal and the patterns on his computer display. His overall results were not as promising as the carefully selected, hindsight-biased examples given during Harry's course or the candlestick course demonstration. The one-hour chart produced a 25 percent win rate, which was not acceptable to Arthur, so next he tried the four-hour chart. This produced a better result of 29 percent, but he knew he could do better. And so he moved to the daily chart. With the daily chart his win rate went to 35 percent, but he knew something was wrong. He had found his sweet spot, but his number of trades went from six hundred on the one-hour chart to twenty-five trades on the daily chart. As a graduate student, Arthur had studied statistical probability, and he knew twenty-five trades was not a good statistical sample.

Banging his head against the computer monitor, Arthur started cursing at himself. He had spent more than 60 percent of his family's savings over the past seven months, and yet he was not making any progress on his trading development. His wife could tell that he was stressed out by his lack of appetite. She knew that his day job was going fine; it was his obsession with trading that was consuming all of his spare time at home and causing him anxiety. Late one Saturday night, his wife came to his desk and consoled him. She told him something that turned out to be a flash of brilliance, and this ultimately led to Arthur's "aha" moment. It was a moment of profound clarity during which he gained real insight that he could use to change his trading approach.

His wife had asked him why he was learning what others already knew. If everyone else knew about it through courses, books, forums, etc., then where was the edge? If he were sick today, would he take penicillin that was invented a hundred years ago? Of course not, thought Arthur. He would take a more effective medicine derived from penicillin. Everything suddenly came together for him. He understood that trading techniques had advanced similarly to medicine and other technologies. For instance, his company was using 3-D facial recognition, which was more accurate than the older 2-D method. He came to realize that too many instructors were still teaching obsolete techniques such as bull and bear candlestick patterns and other useless methods. In order to beat everyone, he had to become a researcher and develop his own trading techniques.

With perseverance, Arthur went back to the one-hour chart to combine the eastern candlestick patterns with the western indicators such as RSI, Stochastic, MACD, and others. The concept was that candlestick patterns helped spot reversal patterns and that there were psychological explanations behind each pattern. Arthur did not want to abandon his candlestick knowledge. He added more filters to make his candlestick patterns work on the one-hour chart. He understood that technical indicators are mathematical formulas applied to the past *n* periods. They were useless by themselves because they could not provide traders with long-term profitable buy or sell signals. If technical indicators could advise how the market would behave in the future *n* periods, all successful FX traders would be good programmers, himself included. Unfortunately, traders love indicators, especially when someone displayed a MACD indicator showing the buy and sell signals of a hindsight-biased chart.

With his obsession to create the right system, first-rate programming skills, and a positive attitude, five months later Arthur was able to make his candlestick patterns work on the one-hour chart. The marriage of eastern and western trading philosophies had yielded some fruitful back-testing results. It was at this point that he went back to his wife with the results of his trading-program development. She was impressed and, though not a numbers person, quickly saw the potential of the approach. Instead of rushing to trade according to the new system with real money, Arthur took his wife's advice and traded on a demo account for two months. It was a good thing he did so because his new system was losing in real-time trading.

One of the strange phenomena Arthur experienced was the "repainting" of his trading program. He would see a buy signal on his screen, and his program would take the trade. However, an hour later, the buy signal would disappear as if the computer had changed its mind, and Arthur was left holding an orphan trade.

There were many other times when trade signals were given, but the market had moved significantly in the other direction. More often than not, entering the trade would not yield the significant profit compared to the back-testing results using his system after the fact. Arthur would leave his computer on for one week and collect all the trades during the entire week. He would then call these transactions his forward-testing results. At the end of the week, he would run the simulation at the beginning to the end of the same week; these transactions were then his back-testing results. There was an extremely low correlation between his back- and forward-testing results.

After three weeks of head banging and hair pulling, Arthur was still unable to determine the errors in his code. When he had come across more complex and more challenging problems at work, he always managed to surmount them. Why should this time be any different? He checked his code again for the hundredth time, and then another "aha" moment came to him. Arthur came to the realization that trading was truly quite complex and that he had to show it more respect. Arthur wondered to himself how many more complex issues he would have to solve before he could conquer the market. Trading was a multifaceted problem. If it were easy, his company could have created trading pattern recognition for the market instead of facial-recognition software to be sold to airports and casinos. Patterns were patterns, and if there were recognizable patterns in the FX market, his company would stand to profit billions. The more Arthur thought about it, the more he hated Harry. It was a scam to claim it was easy to make money in the FX market.

Arthur discovered that all the indicators and candlestick patterns in his system were set up incorrectly—they defaulted to the close price, which is why indicators show extremely promising results on historical charts but perform inadequately in real-time trading. The candlestick formation is based on open, high, low, and close prices. An example is the stock market—if the market opens today at 9:00 a.m., we come in knowing only yesterday's open, high, low, and close prices. We won't know the market's high, low, and close prices until the end of the day. The only price that we know in real time is the open price of the market. Back-testing software does not know any better. It calculates results based on known data at the time when the back testing is performed. It is up to the user to set the price calculation to "open" to avoid this hindsight bias. This is a more realistic approach because only at the end of the day would we be able to know the high, low, and close prices of the day. The disturbing fact is that all charting software programs in the market have their indicators defaulted to the close price. This setting automatically makes indicators like RSI, MACD, and CCI appear more accurate. It is even more unfortunate that most traders don't realize this discrepancy in settings exists.

• • •

Michelle's Story

Michelle was the last member of the gang of seven. Just twenty-three, she was the youngest of the group. She was also a recent graduate of the University of Chicago, where she had majored in history. Michelle had become aware of Harry's FX trading course when she had applied for a job handing out flyers for his trading school. He was looking for attractive females for the job and was paying them twenty-five dollars an hour to hand out flyers in various parts of Chicago. At the time, Michelle had just graduated from school and needed a job, any sort of job, to help pay her rent. She shared an apartment with two other girls who were in much the same situation. In fact, the way she had learned about Harry's job was through one of her roommates who had been doing it for a while and said that it was easy money.

Michelle never had any exposure to the financial markets, or trading, for that matter. She didn't have the slightest idea what any of it was about and really didn't care either. She was just trying to get by as best as she could. Her last boyfriend had graduated three years before and had taken a journalist job with a newspaper in California. Though they had pledged their undying love to each other before parting and that they would visit each other every month, that vision lasted all of three months. After that, both of them knew that the long-distance relationship thing was no good for either of them, and each eventually started dating other people.

Michelle was the most attractive of her girlfriends. She stood five feet eight and had beautiful, naturally blonde hair, as she was, like many of the citizens of Wisconsin, of Scandinavian descent. As a child and into her teens, she had been active in gymnastics, and this had molded her body into that of a gorgeously fit athlete. She had long legs, a small waist, pert bosom, and a golden tan she worked on year-round. Her smile was radiant, a testament to her parents' investment in orthodontia, but her most striking feature was her eyes, which were the most stunning shade of blue. Michelle was well aware of her physical gifts and used them to get what she wanted, especially from men, who never ceased to give her special attention. She was, quite simply, a stunning physical specimen.

Her looks were both a virtue and a vice. As much as she enjoyed the excessive attention she effortlessly garnered, Michelle felt her looks did her a disservice at times. Beauty is often associated with brainlessness, and this stereotype frustrated Michelle. She liked to be perceived as a smart, independent, and responsible individual, not just a pretty face. She constantly endeavored to establish herself as a force to be reckoned with, and when most everyone expected her to stand still and look pretty, she grew more determined. Michelle looked for an outlet that would allow her to demonstrate her potential. She was driven to no end and wanted to sink her teeth into something meaningful and challenging.

When she appeared for the interview, it was a foregone conclusion that Harry would hire her. In fact, Harry took one look at Michelle and was totally enchanted. He would have given her anything she asked for he was so love-struck. She, of course, knew this, as it was a common occurrence in her dealings with men. Men just could not resist her charms. And so Harry gave her the job on the spot. He also gave her the best location in town to work. He also remarked to her, “If things work out, I’m sure I can find a more suitable position for you in my organization.” Once again, Michelle’s beauty had proven itself advantageous, and she did not mind it as long as it helped her fulfill her ambitions.

But she was determined to prove her brains were the bigger advantage. Looking over the flyers she was handing out, Michelle became curious about the claims Harry made in his ads. Was it really true that you could make money from trading this FX thing? Why hadn’t she heard about it before now if this was such a sure thing? This had to be marketing hype, she thought. Then one afternoon, about a week after she started working for Harry, she had a lengthy conversation with him about all the claims he was making in his handouts. At the back of her mind, she pondered the possibility that FX trading would be that outlet to show that she was more than just a pretty face. After answering her questions, Harry suggested that she attend one of his free seminars and see what she thought. Michelle went to the next seminar, and though she had never even taken a business course at school, she was impressed by Harry's presentation and explanation of trading concepts as well as the FX markets and their potential for new traders. She was convinced that this was something she could do and make money at. Maybe she would even be able to support herself full time trading FX. She knew that she might not get another chance this good to prove her potential and be taken seriously, so she jumped at the opportunity.

The only problem for Michelle was that she was flat broke. She had no way of coming up with the $1,500 course tuition. It might as well have been $1.5 million as far as she was concerned. When Harry asked if she was interested in taking his course, she told him that she would love to but she didn't have the money. Harry not only offered her a discount of $1,000 since she was one of his employees, but he would allow her to pay him in installments. Overjoyed with this news, Michelle enrolled for the next course, where she met the other members of the gang of seven. She too kept in touch with the group, and they all shared their systems and results on a daily and weekly basis. Some members of the group were more active than others, but everyone participated. Michelle found that she was now very interested in seeing what the various markets were doing, and she began to piece together how certain economic events would influence the direction of the FX market specifically.

Michelle found it extremely difficult to execute trades because she was constantly second-guessing herself. However, she found that it was easy to analyze market behavior, and, like most analysts, she was very good at providing post-game breakdowns. For instance, if oil prices were rising, she could tell that the US dollar and the Japanese yen were going to fall because they depended heavily on imported oil. If Britain raised its interest rate, she could tell that the pound would strengthen because institutional investors would shift their assets to it to gain higher returns. If there were a decrease in the payroll employment, she would be able to make the connection of weak economic activity that could eventually lead to lower interest rates and a decrease in the price of that currency. Her go-to answer for when a currency was not behaving according to the news release was that the market had already priced it in. She could always come up with a plausible explanation for why the market did what it did. Unfortunately, like many trading instructors, currency analysts, and currency strategists, she was unable to predict what would happen next. And yet many traders still flock to such analysts for guidance. If analysts could consistently predict what would happen next in the markets, they would become hedge fund managers and multibillionaires. Most analysts' recommendations are not tracked over time for profitability or accuracy.

Although she followed the major FX currency pairs, Michelle took the advice of one of her classmates who suggested that it was best to keep things simple when starting out by focusing on only one pair, and that pair should be the EUR/USD because of its high trading volume. Michelle also became a voracious reader of books, magazines, and trading forums having anything to do with FX trading. She had been a good student in college and made very good grades. She attributed much of this to the fact that her exams were generally of the open-book variety, and, unlike her fellow students who would cart four or five books into the exam room, Michelle boiled down the course readings by condensing them into summaries that she would fit onto one standard, typewritten page per book.

Her ability to pinpoint the most important information gave Michelle a distinct advantage over her classmates, as most people remember only 5 percent of what they read. By condensing the information in her books into a summary of key points, she was able to answer her exam questions comprehensively, which is how Michelle aced most of her college courses. She followed the same approach with her trading book information—she would take notes during her reading and then condense them down to a letter-sized page per book. At first, she would take notes on five-inch index cards, which she kept in an index card box, but she found that it took several index cards per book, and her card box was getting overstuffed. She switched to a three-ring binder, with each page containing the most critical points of each book, very simple to consult for trading information and fundamental analyses. Easy and quick access to this information helped her to assess potential trade setups and review her contents in the most efficient way.

Many traders make the mistake of assuming that once they understand a new concept in a trading book, they have the key to trading success. This new information becomes a part of their personality. Many claim that they have read more than fifty trading books; however, few can recall the three most important points from each book. Knowledge does not automatically translate to competence. There are four levels of competence, and the first level is unconscious incompetence:

we do not know what we don't know. We may not necessarily recognize or may even deny the usefulness of the skill. The second level is conscious incompetence: we know what we don't know. We recognize the deficit, and we need to learn new skills to overcome the deficit. Most traders read books to move toward the third level, conscious competence, only to fall back to the second level. In order to maintain the level of conscious competence, we need to attempt, experiment, and practice. There is still a high level of concentration involved in executing this new skill, even though we understand or know how to do something. Most traders are too lazy to review and practice what they have learned. With her concise notes, Michelle was able to review what she had learned so that she could constantly practice it. Unfortunately, people tend not to take notes when they read. After so much practice, a skill will become second nature, to the point that it can be performed while executing another task. Unfortunately, most traders are unable to achieve this last level: unconscious competence.

Michelle concluded one day that being a fundamentally good trader was not enough. To be successful, a trader needed ample capital and at least three to four years to really get into the markets, which to her meant being a full-time trader. How could she possibly do this when she was barely able to pay her rent? Michelle had read many trading books, and she noticed something in particular. One author was a full-time doctor, and trading was his second job. Trading may have been his passion, but being a doctor would provide him with steady income to pursue his dreams. In another trading book, the author had a rich father who allowed him to live rent-free in a beautiful cabin while he performed his day trading. Most authors and educators in one way or another another inspired their readers and students to trade full time. Ironically, these authors themselves did not, and most of their income came from their training courses, forum subscriptions, and other materials. Michelle recognized that trading full time was a privilege, and, therefore, she needed to find other ways to generate income. Was a sugar daddy the answer to her problem?

To become a successful trader, it is important to have ample time and financial resources. You must have someone supporting you or have enough funds to cover your living expenses for at least several years. There is enormous stress involved in trading, and the stress will become impossible to deal with if you are depending on your trading profits to cover your monthly expenses. You should trade only with money you don't need to live on. Unfortunately, trading educators will not disclose these facts because they depend on your tuition fees to pay for their lavish lifestyles.

SUMMARY OF CHAPTER 5

1. Trading is not for everyone.

Highly impulsive personalities with the need to see quick action can find trading an overwhelming experience. They are prone to making poor trading decisions because their impulsive nature clouds any proper judgment and impedes any effort to stay disciplined. It is not an easy process to change one's personality—it is a long, arduous journey. If you cannot overcome those behavioral patterns that are not conducive to trading, it is best not to trade at all.

2. Taking a five-day workshop will not transform you into a successful trader overnight.

Short-term educational experiences are not likely to change your trading habits. Research has shown that, on average, it takes a minimum of sixty-six days and as long as 254 days of dedication and commitment to establish a good habit in place of a bad one. However, most traders will need at least five years of concerted effort to rid themselves of their multiple bad habits (since it is rarely just one they have developed).

3. **The financial trading industry progresses just like any field.**

All areas and disciplines advance and progress, yet too many FX trading instructors are still teaching obsolete techniques such as bull and bear candlestick patterns and other overused, and even proven useless, indicators. If an indicator has been around for years and has been commoditized to the masses, what edge would you gain by using it? You would be using the same techniques everybody else is using, and you would be subject to the same pitfalls.

4. **Technical indicators are mathematical formulas applied to the last *n* periods.**

The oldest bromide in trading is that past performance is not indicative of future performance, yet technical indicators are fundamentally built on the last *n* period (historical information). The trick is uncovering the next *n* periods, not building upon the last *n* periods and using them as a benchmark to predict the market. If technical indicators could uncover how the market would behave in the next *n* periods, mammoth profits from FX trading would not be so hard to achieve.

5. All indicators are defaulted at the close price.

There is a reason why indicators show extremely promising results on historical charts but perform inadequately in real-time trading; they are based on close price. Indicators should use the open price to eliminate "repainting" because in real time we know only the opening price and not the high, low, or close of the market.

6. Analysts cannot uncover the Holy Grail.

Most of the time, analysts know just as much as the next person. If they could consistently predict how the market would perform, you best believe they would not be working as analysts. They would opt for the millions that could be profited from working as hedge fund managers. The track record of analysts' predictions proves their inefficacy, but rarely do we have the attention span to keep following it.

7. Success in trading requires ample time and resources.

You must have someone supporting you or have enough funds to cover your expenses for at least several years if you want to venture into trading full time. There is enormous stress involved in trading, and the stress level will become impossible to deal with if you are depending on your trading profits to cover your monthly expenses. Otherwise, you would be opening up yourself to enormous stress that will only hinder your trading and ultimately put you through losses.

8. Identify your trading edge.

Ron's trading edge is that he is coming in with lots of trading capital. Arthur's trading edge is his programming skills, attitude, and perseverance. Michelle's edge is her analytical competence and her understanding of time and resources. What trading edge are you bringing with you to the FX market?

CHAPTER 6

DAVID VERSUS THE FX BROKER GOLIATH

The waves lapped upon the shores of the British Virgin Islands, a tropical paradise found at the edge of the Caribbean Sea—a hub for tourists, who skinny-dipped in the warm water, and for business owners like Robert, who didn't always want to play by the rules and saw the islands as a no-holds-barred playground.

Robert stared out his office window, looking at the beautiful turquoise waters of the Caribbean. The sky was a deep, cloudless blue, and there was a slight breeze blowing onshore. It was a wonderful day for sailing, but Robert would not be able to take his fifty-seven-foot Catalina sailboat out due to the demands of his FX brokerage business. Eight years ago, Robert left New York, where he had started up his FX brokerage, taking advantage of the newly deregulated commodity futures industry. It proved to be a gold mine for brokerage houses that geared themselves toward the small retail FX trader. The profit margin was amazing, and the risk factors were relatively controllable.

Unfortunately, the federal regulators imposed ever-increasing capital and other requirements on the retail FX industry, which forced many small firms to relocate offshore where they would not be subject to US laws and regulations. Seeing the writing on the wall, Robert also relocated his entire operation to Road Town in the British Virgin Island of Tortola. This spot was ideal for Robert because it allowed him to pursue two of the things he loved the most: running his trading business and sailing the Caribbean. The picture was not all rosy, as there were the usual drawbacks. For instance, Robert disliked the food available on the island. A main food staple of this part of the Caribbean was something known as "fungi," which consisted of cornmeal and okra boiled and cooked together until it reached a thick consistency. The dish never appealed to Robert. There was an abundance of seafood to be had, but Robert was never a big fish eater, as much as his wife tried to get him to eat it for his health. One could get some decent cuts of beef, but it was extraordinarily expensive, and the supply was always spotty.

Robert missed his native California, with its diverse cultures and fabulous restaurants. But his life was now in the islands since he moved his FX business there. In the good old days, immediately after the deregulation of the FX market in 2000, Robert had been a very successful FX trader working for Deutsch Bank in New York. He and others immediately saw the potential of attracting the small retail traders to this new market. Back then, the capital requirements for his firm were only at $1 million, and his company thrived with new FX traders. His firm offered leverage as high as 400:1, and clients could open an account with as little as $250. He quickly grew his firm's revenue from $500,000 to $5 million over a period of three years. Instead of operating like a traditional broker, i.e., earning the revenue from the spread on currency pairs, many small FX firms like Robert's switched to being market makers with their limited working capital. Market markers kept all their client trades in inventory to benefit from the fact that historically the majority of retail trading accounts were losers.

With too many small brokers going under due to insufficient capital, the federal Commodity Futures Trading Commission (CFTC) gradually began to increase broker capital requirements from $1 million to $25 million over a period of several years. The CFTC regulates commodity futures and options, and this includes the FX industry. The CTFC is responsible for protecting customers who use these markets and monitors the markets to detect and prevent manipulation. As the broker capital requirement was increased, this forced many of the smaller brokers to quit the business. Instead of closing up shop, Robert relocated his firm to the British Virgin Islands, where his firm would no longer fall under the regulation of the US authorities, and, consequently, his firm would not need to maintain the capital required for US firms. Many other small FX firms moved to Cyprus, Greece, Panama, and Belize for the same reasons.

Looking out his office window onto the tropical greenery, Robert frequently reminisced about the days he operated in the United States. He had prided himself on his army of mercenary lawyers, who continually found ways around rules and regulations. Moving his FX brokerage firm to Tortola was based on his lawyer's recommendation. Ironically, his firm was one of the early few that played by the rules and registered with National Futures Association (NFA), a US trade group. The NFA is a nongovernmental body composed of futures brokers who voluntarily joined and committed to adhering to the organization's rules and regulations, including its capitalization requirements. The NFA regulates the futures brokerage business as a voluntary association—it knows the industry much better than the CFTC does and is better qualified to act as a watchdog. Some of the rules the NFA came up with to try to safeguard the trading public from unscrupulous brokers were to require various reports to be filed on a monthly, quarterly, and annual basis, somewhat similar to the SEC reporting requirements that public companies have to follow. At that time, not all FX brokers had to register with the NFA and abide by its rules. Robert strongly believed that this requirement was going to change sooner or later, as his firm and many similar brokerage firms were making too much money. Robert recognized that the good times would end at some point because the FX brokerage industry was plagued with abuses due to greedy brokers.

One of Robert's research analysts was drilling down customer account information and noticed that only a small percentage of the accounts at the firm were over $20,000. Most of the 25,000 accounts at the firm were in the $250 to $20,000 range. The analyst recommended changing the way the firm handled and processed orders for its customers' accounts. What he proposed was that the firm take the opposite side of all customer accounts under $10,000. In essence, these trades would be inventoried on the firm's trading books, since the firm made very little revenue based on the trading spread on these accounts. Since the industry average was that 92 percent of all retail FX trades ended in a loss to the trader, it seemed that the laws of probability were in his firm's favor by holding these trades internally. Instead of earning the measly spread on these small trades, they were almost guaranteed to pocket all of the small client accounts. Whenever new clients signed up, they voluntary provided their personal data, such as how long they had been trading FX and how much experience they had speculating with stocks and options. Some of this data is required by the regulators; however, Robert's firm used the data to select which client accounts to trade against. Robert's firm exercised caution when playing against client accounts that met or exceeded one of the following conditions: more than $10,000 in the account, five or more years of trading experience, annual income greater than $250,000, and liquid assets greater than $1 million. It was a no-brainer to go after the poorer and more inexperienced traders. His firm did not want to pick on rich clients that might have the resources to hire lawyers to sue the firm. The firm was like a bully in the schoolyard, preying only on easy targets.

For the more sophisticated clients and accounts greater than $10,000, his firm would take these trades to the market as an STP—or straight-through processing—broker. This meant his firm would pass the customer buy and sell orders directly to one or several parties of the interbank market who become the counterparty to the customer's trade. His firm would take only the spread on this type of trade and would not hold it in its own inventory. For large trades like these, the firm would lay off the risk to the market, where the customer would normally get a better price and spread. Robert's firm could still play all of the standard broker tricks but would have less incentive to try to beat the customer because it didn't hold the trade in its inventory.

Firms like Robert's are known as hybrid brokers. Hybrid brokers are the market maker for small clients and an STP for its more sophisticated and larger clients. Robert's firm kept the small trades that had a low probability of success and laid off the large trades that would generate too much exposure if taken on as a market maker. This was not Robert's original revenue model because he was strictly focusing on the STP revenue. It was a combination of having the necessary technology as well as the backing of his analyst, who guided him toward the path of larger revenue with limited risks. Trading against the customer was a highly profitable and legal activity that became a main source of revenue for his firm.

Robert always got a big grin on his face whenever a new client opened up a trading account with $250 and selected the maximum leverage of 400:1. Here comes another idiot hoping to turn $250 into $1 million by the end of the year, he thought. FX firms like Robert's did well because of trading schools like Harry's that promised unlimited gains from trading and the possibility of trading full time for a living. Robert considered the majority of his clients embarrassingly naïve for falling for marketing scams such as ten pips a day, compounding trading lots each month, and other so-called tricks that were in reality flat-out lies. People never realized that trading was not for everyone and that some reasonable affinity for the process was required. Could a "normal" person make $10,000 per month without having a real job, relying solely on FX trading?

"Don't these people realize they're being taken in?" Robert's analyst asked.

"If they did, you'd be out of a job. Our clients are naïve, gullible people who signed up based on false hope," Robert said, smirking. "But I'm not complaining. Their stupidity has made me very successful."

Robert was glad that he did not have to deal directly with his clients, whom he unashamedly perceived and treated as idiots. Maybe one day, he could write a memoir about his life and thank all his clients for foolishly trading with their money. For example, even the most educated and experienced traders would fool themselves by creating a false trading plan that had $10,000 as starting capital. For these clients, the order of their trading plan priorities was generally capital preservation first and foremost, followed by capital accumulation, and last, income. They would risk no more than 2 percent per trade but would attempt to compound their winnings monthly. Their goals were to accumulate $27,100 by the end of the first year and $44,200 by the end of the second year. They claimed that they were not greedy and would start withdrawing $1,000 per month only after their account reached $50,000. Robert had to give credit to operations like Harry's because they promoted hope and inspiration for the little guys. By instilling hope surrounding the potential to become a trading millionaire, FX coaches and mentors like Harry provided optimism to the poor, the gamblers, the unemployed, the inexperienced, and the down and out. However, the more intelligent students would be wary about turning a $10,000 account into $27,000 in a year since that amounted to a 170 percent return. By emphasizing that they would only be risking 2 percent of their total account per trade and should only look for a 5 to 10 percent return per month on their capital, the math to turn $10,000 into $27,000 in a year became a lot easier. The monthly compounding trick works every time. Previously, investment returns were counted in years, but now they are counted in months.

Robert explained to his wife that FX trading was a legalized form of gambling and that his firm simply provided a portal for his customers. His wife hated the idea, but Robert always explained to her that he wasn't doing anything illegal. It was all a matter of supply and demand. If he did not offer the service, someone else would. He also regularly donated 10 percent of his net profits to her favorite charities as a peace offering. Robert reasoned that most women would prefer a rich husband over a poor husband with ethical values. Ethical values would not pay for her expensive tastes in luxury vacations, designer clothes, opulent homes, rare wines, fine dining, and diamond jewelry. She got a lot of attention from different charity organizations that treated her like royalty as long as she kept making contributions. She began to have the delusional idea that she was somehow contributing to society and making the world a better place. Her charitable ventures allowed them to mingle with the upper crust of society, and they were regularly invited to all the best social events. They were considered to be among the who's who of society. All the while, his wife was fully aware that her husband was a far cry from a philanthropist and that his money was not very clean.

Robert's firm had a standard bag of tricks that it used to get its clients' money. This seemed to be a sure-fire way to increase the firm's profitability with limited risks. It was well known that the vast majority of the brokers played fast and loose with their clients, and Robert's firm was no exception. When his firm first started in business, the spread for the EUR/USD currency pair was as high as three pips. When more and more FX brokerage firms got into the business, they started to compete viciously to decrease the spread. At first, all the demo accounts were defaulted to $5,000, but soon new firms would come in offering $10,000 or $25,000 demo accounts. Then some firms started advertising $50,000 demo accounts. It didn't make any difference because the small-time traders would never see their accounts with that many zeros anyway. Robert did not mind such marketing tactics because it did not cost him anything to change the default setting of the firm's demo accounts. Nevertheless, his firm's revenues decreased significantly when other brokers started to undercut each other by offering two-pip spreads and some as low as 1.2 pips for the EUR/USD. Every broker was lowering his spreads, hoping to have an edge over the others. What they didn't realize was that this was a race to the bottom. In a highly competitive environment, these brokers were competing strictly on price instead of offering customers value. Robert knew that nobody wins a race to bottom. However, his brokerage firm had to meet the competition and was forced to lower its spreads to compete.

With narrower spreads came lower revenues for Robert's firm, and he needed new ways to squeeze his current clients and find more ways to attract new ones. Squeezing new clients was easy since there were several dozen ways of increasing an FX brokerage firm's profitability. One of the most famous ways of gaming an FX customer's account was by "stop running" or "stop tripping." This is a practice of manipulating the price of the market data feed. Robert's firm could set its price-feed spike (also known as price injection) to catch a large number of stop-loss orders that were clustered around various price levels on his firm's trading chart system. Since market movements happen in a milliseconds, his firm could claim that there was a momentary blip in price activity that took out a client's stop loss. The firm could always see where all of its clients' stop losses were sitting. He could also filter out by currency pair and account size. If there was a significant cluster around certain price levels on a certain currency pair, his firm would do everything in its power to try to get its price feed to hit those stops and take the customers out of their trades at a loss to the customers. Robert had trained his customer representatives to explain to clients that there was a temporary low liquidity in the market causing prices to spike and vice versa. Robert resorted to these cons out of necessity as he had business expenses to pay to keep his firm afloat. It was about survival, and he had to do whatever it took to be a good provider for his wife and his employees, whose lives obviously depended on their jobs.

A second method of fleecing the customer is known as "widening the spread." Most brokerage firms do not guarantee fixed spreads at two pips or 1.2 pips for the EUR/USD since FX is a fast-moving market. During very active times of the market, the the spread can be as large as three to ten pips. Robert's firm and any other broker can automatically widen their spread as much as ten pips or more. This allowed them to pocket the difference as profits. Clients would always be paying much more than the advertised teaser rate of, say, two pips. Most new traders didn't know better and would select an FX broker based on whichever one was offering the lowest spread. All brokers have different internal algorithms for their variable and fixed spreads on all the major currency pairs. Many new FX traders believe that a fixed spread is better than a variable spread. However, some brokers claim that it is better to choose a variable-spread FX broker if they don't trade during major news releases or the low-trading volume periods. Few newbie FX traders are aware of the fact that a broker's advertised spread is only a marketing tool and that it is not the best practice to compare spread prices as a basis for selecting an FX broker. Robert's firm, for instance, had specially designed software to ensure that clients would pay adequately for their spread in one way or another.

The third method brokers use to take advantage of their customers is known as "slippage" in price, and it can occur during fast markets or poor liquidity. When the market moves really fast, clients will not get their orders filled at the price they see quoted. By the time a customer's order has hit the market, prices may have moved away from where the customer thought his or her order had been filled. Robert's firm, as a matter of standard practice, would add a few additional slippage pips in its favor if a customer was willing to get the position at the higher pip spread. His firm would always make slippage work in their favor regardless of market conditions. For instance, a customer places a sell order for the EUR/USD at 1.3008, and by the time Robert's firm executes the order, the rate has changed to 1.3000. The client would not get the lower price; the additional eight pips was profit for the firm. Robert's firm could also manipulate stop-loss slippages. For instance, with a buy stop loss set at 1.2535, his firm could cause the stop loss to slip to 1.2530, resulting in an additional five pips' loss to the client. The standard response is that there was a strong market movement for this new price level. There is an asymmetrical slippage practice whereby the market movement will always work against the client and never to his advantage. Robert's clients always paid more than their stop losses for strong market movement when the market was going against their trades. However, whenever there was a strong market movement in the customers' favor, their profit order would always be filled exactly. This was because any additional profitable slippage would be pocketed by Robert's brokerage firm. All brokerage firms practice price slippage, but Robert had set an internal operating procedure so that it was not too detrimental to his customers. His view was that if you cheat too much, your customers will be onto you. If you cheat sporadically, then it is easier to get away with it. Similar to poker, a good player must bluff once in a while. It is a necessary technique to win the hand, but you are more likely to get caught if you overuse it.

Robert also used a method known as "price shading," whereby his firm would assess the incoming order flow, determining whether there were more customers interested in buying or selling. If his firm saw more retail orders going to the "buy side," the firm would charge his buying customers more than the quoted actual price being offered in the interbank market. The buyer pays a little more, and his firm increases its profit.

Next was the method called "shilling." With this method, the customer is tricked by using disproportionate swaps, also known as "overnight interest rates." If a trader holds a trade overnight, his brokerage firm charges him an interest rate. The broker will charge and pay overnight swaps on currency pairs depending on the difference between the short-term interest rates associated with the central banks of the countries of the currencies involved. The brokerage firm charges a higher interest rate to the trader than required by the firm's swap counterpart. In the case that the broker pays out the swap, it would always pay out less than required. For most small accounts and trades, i.e., retail trades, the broker will never go to the swap market to hedge the overnight trade, but will hold it in its inventory, yet still charge the customer as if it had gone out to the market to hedge his or her trade overnight.

Robert's firm created a house advantage over its customers by setting the default in his client's leverage position to 400:1, thus encouraging larger trade volumes. If a client had $1,000 cash in his or her 400:1 margin account, he or she could purchase up to $400,000 worth of currency since he or she had to post only 0.25 percent of the purchase price as collateral. By offering such a huge leverage position to his customers, Robert increased the chances that they would make impulsive and irrational trades. When coupled with the fact that it would be unlikely that the average trader would pull all his or her winnings out of his or her account versus continuing to trade with his or her newly enlarged pot, Robert had statistically proven that the risk to his firm was almost nonexistent. With increased leverage, the likelihood of his customers overtrading and losing their entire accounts was greatly increased.

Robert's next method relied on delaying his customers' trade execution time so that the firm could gain from late responses. This method is a variation of the slippage in price practice, but the difference is that it is based on time delays to cause slippage in price. By delaying the trade execution time by three to five seconds, clients were given the worst possible entry price for the trade, and Robert's firm pocketed the difference. Since FX is a fast-moving market, execution time is counted in milliseconds. A delay of a few seconds is more than one thousand times slower than the typical transaction, which takes one millisecond. By delaying the trade order by a few seconds, the market may move against clients by many pips, which means more profits for Robert's firm. However, there is an asymmetry betting against a firm's customers. If during the delay the market moved in favor of the customer, this positive gain was always capped at a few pips so that it posed little risk to Robert's firm.

When it came to marketing his firm, Robert cleverly did so by marketing it as a "no dealing desk" brokerage. This was simply another method of tricking his clients. For "dealing desk" brokers, there is a person on the other side of the trade. A broker involved in both sides of a transaction creates a substantial conflict of interest because the broker has a vested interest to see his clients lose. The dealing-desk broker needs to manually approve every trade that comes through. If there are hundreds and hundreds of trades coming in, there tend to be long delays and slippages. In a no dealing-desk environment, the computer automatically matches the order, and this is done almost instantaneously, in milliseconds. Technically, this was true for Robert's firm because there wasn't a human-operated dealing desk. Instead, his company used a software dealing-desk application to manipulate and interfere with customer trades.

Robert's other trick involved blocking his customers' winning trades. On the smaller retail customer accounts, where his firm was the market maker, every winning customer trade resulted in a loss to his company. It was in the firm's best interest to see that those trades didn't win or that his customers' take-profit orders were not executed. To achieve this, his firm could route the trades to "slow" servers or send out false error messages when his customers attempted to close out profitable trades. He would allow clients to exit profitable trades only after the market had somewhat retracted. This minimized customers' winning trades and simultaneously the potential losses to his firm.

Robert's firm had also recently purchased a software program that allowed him to modify any of his customers' trades and orders, including entry price, stop-loss, and take-profit positions. All Robert had to do was select the client order number and then change any of the elements of trade order to whatever he wanted. Any adjustments that he made were not logged, and most of his clients were not very good record keepers. Minor changes to the entry price and stop loss provided additional revenue for his company. Even if the customers noticed some suspicious activities, the changes were so small that it would be unlikely the issue would transform into a conflict contested in court.

Another method used by Robert's firm was the "occasional" re-quote. In this situation, his brokerage firm would not execute a customer trade at the price where the customer wanted to enter the market. Generally, when a customer decided to buy or sell a currency pair at a particular price and pressed the button to submit the order, within milliseconds the firm received the order. Robert's staff could then manually accept or reject any order coming from a customer. Most of the time, all the incoming orders were handled on an automated basis by the firm's computer server. However, there was a special application that could be launched to process trades manually. Robert's senior team could reject a customer's order by sending an "off quote" message or by replying with a re-quote announcement, letting the client know that the price had moved beyond his or her order price.

The re-quote would, of course, always be a price that was worse than the one the customer ordered. Robert's customer orders were truly at the mercy of his firm. Most of the firm's staff were unaware of the software application since it was used only by the senior members of his team. At times, there were legitimate reasons for some re-quotes, such as when the market moved extremely fast, and it could move even more quickly during news announcements. An example of the latter is during the Non-Farm Payroll report announcement that comes out the first Friday of each month. Conveniently, all Robert had to do if a customer complained was to say that his interbank brokers that provided the liquidity pool for his firm's trades were responsible for the re-quote, in which case it was virtually impossible for a customer to prove otherwise. The blame game was a classic defense. Most clients have to live with this chicanery since they are given the opportunity to decide whether or not to accept the new but inferior price.

Also in the firm's arsenal of weapons is a history-changing tool that can edit any chart history price candle such as the high, low, open, close, and volume. Few traders know that all historical FX prices are susceptible to editing, and it is a handy tool for an FX broker to "fix up" prices after stop-loss hunting. Since FX is a noncentralized exchange, chart price manipulation is a free-for-all operation at brokerage firms. Originally, these types of tools were created to fix price glitches or system issues. Unfortunately, the temptation to the FX broker community is uncontrollable, and these tools are used instead to increase a broker's profitability.

Most online services claim a 99.9 percent uptime, but there are many variations on how they calculate this number. Unfortunately, most FX brokerage firms do not have a similar guarantee for their broker server connection. When a customer opened up an FX account with Robert's firm, they were required to sign an electronic trading agreement with a limitation of liability to the firm that stated that the customer could not hold the broker liable for trade failures in the event of server disconnections. This allows the FX broker to merely "turn off" his or her trading server at certain times during a trading session when the market is highly volatile or when a customer has a big trade that is going against the broker. This disconnection prevents clients from exiting their profitable trade until the market retraces to a broker's more favorable point or causes a failure of a customer's trade execution altogether. When this occurs, the disconnection minimizes the customer's profit as well as causes havoc on systematic trading systems, otherwise known as "expert advisors" or robot-trading systems.

In Robert's firm, not every customer was treated the same. For large client accounts, a separate and speedier trading server known as the "Rich Daddy" was used. These big accounts always received preferential treatment, from quicker and more consistent price quoting to quicker market execution and straight-through processing. Since these accounts were fewer, the firm's dedicated big account server was never running on more than 15 percent capacity. As for smaller micro and mini accounts (which made up the bulk of Robert's firm), they all went onto two trading servers known as "Dreamer" and "Hopeful." These servers were always running at 95 percent of CPU memory capacity. Since more and more small accounts were opened up, these two servers were constantly running at their maximum capacity. The result was slower and more sporadic price quotes and reduced trade execution time. If a customer ran an automated systematic trading system on two separate accounts at Robert's firm, one on the "Rich Daddy" and another on either the "Dreamer" or "Hopeful" server, he or she would never get the same trading results. The trading account on "Rich Daddy" always got a consistent and stable data feed, which was extremely critical for systematic trading, whereas the account on "Dreamer" would receive erratic price feeds resulting in poor input data. In the world of systematic trading, this is known as "GIGO"—garbage in, garbage out.

Most FX brokers use other cheating techniques as well, including unfilled orders and account banning, just to name a couple. But Robert's favorite trick was the forced margin call. His firm adopted a practice whereby on the last Friday of each month, the brokers would lower the leverage on all smaller client accounts from 400:1 leverage to 100:1. This end-of-month adjustment would increase a customer's margin requirement from 0.25 percent to 1 percent. Since most new traders tended to hold onto their large losing positions, their positions would be immediately liquidated. Robert's lawyers advised him on several "plausible deniability" techniques that would provide several layers of insulation from customer lawsuits. According to his lawyers, Robert's worst-case scenario would be failing to supervise his trading platform and/or failing to supervise the firm's operations. His lawyers told him that at most he would be fined, but he would not have to admit or deny the charges. Robert was a great trader in his own right because he always calculated his risks and had his stop loss in place. The great thing about all of this was that implementing all of these tricks happened during the six years that his firm was located in the United States. Now that his firm was in the British Virgin Islands, he had even less to fear.

Robert had heard of rumors that the NFA was going to request a monthly and quarterly report on the number of winning accounts from each FX broker. Although he no longer had to put up with the NFA requirements, he was quite certain that many of his competitor firms in the United States would find ways to neuter that rule. Brokers merely added a few cents of "interest" to their many dormant accounts, so they could quickly increase the number of profitable accounts. Since many customers who stop trading never formally close out their accounts when they have only a small balance left, there are many dormant accounts that the brokers can use to game the NFA's rules. There was a constant influx of new FX accounts being opened, and a firm could strategically delay clients from trading their new accounts by one or two days. Depending on when the report was taken, a break-even or no-trade account can be considered a winning account. There are clients who open up trading accounts but never deposit any funds. FX firms can also tally these accounts as winning accounts. The bottom line is that an army of industry lawyers would lobby the NFA for ways that allow their brokerage firm clients to get around the methodology of how their profitable accounts are calculated. The FX brokerage industry has too much at stake.

In the FX industry, a common term is lifetime value (LTV). The average LTV for FX traders is about six to ten months, and the average account loss is $3,000, according to the FX Magnates 2012 report. Some brokers claim that their customers have the highest percentage of profitable accounts, based on the

CFTC-required reporting. However, these numbers show only a snapshot of profitability during that specific quarter only and not over a longer period. Had it been required to show profitability over a year and not a quarter, the numbers would probably be far worse. Also, the CFTC shows only the percentage of clients with profitable versus unprofitable accounts. So if 70 percent of the clients were up by one dollar, but 30 percent of the clients lost 99 percent of their money, the report would still show 70 percent of the clients as having profited. Imagine there are a hundred accounts, and seventy accounts win one dollar each; the total gain is $70. Meanwhile the thirty accounts lose $99 each; the total loss is $2,970. The brokers will proudly state that they have 70 percent winning accounts according to the CFTC-required reporting. They will go to great lengths to discredit the statistic that 92 percent of FX traders lose money.

Robert dreamed that one day he would write a book that would be a compilation of his tricks of the trade. However, after consulting with his lawyers, they advised him against the project—it would open him up to possible legal liability since it might be viewed as an admission of wrongdoing on his part. These little tricks might not seem like much, but when multiplied by numerous customer accounts day in and day out, over time it adds up to a substantial amount of ill-gained profit. Who could challenge these practices? FX trading is not centralized, and all the information is in the sole control of the brokerage firms. There have been many regulatory actions taken against most of the big retail FX brokers for pulling these tricks on their customers, but the net effect on the small client is minimal. The brokerage firms get slapped with a fine and promise to improve their procedure and processes, but none of them would have to admit to any wrongdoing. Robert and his lawyers discussed these issues at great length, and he even budgeted for fines and legal fees as part of his firm's operational expenses. The cardinal rule for any firm was never to get caught committing the same crime twice because the punishment is exceptionally severe in that case. In fact, most customer complaints never ripen into lawsuits. A small retail trader with a $500 or a $5,000 account that was taken by a broker's shenanigans would never be able to recover his or her money. He or she would spend much more pursuing a lawsuit than he or she could ever hope to receive, even if he or she won. The brokerage houses all know this and have teams of big, expensive lawyers on retainer to protect them from such lawsuits. It's a case of David against Goliath, and here Goliath always wins. The cruel reality is that brokers factor in the cost of paying fines and defending lawsuits in their business models, and to them, it is just another cost of doing business.

Reading the daily newspaper, Robert noticed that several high-profile FX brokerage firms in the United States had been fined by the NFA. New York IKON Global Market was fined $320,000, New Jersey Gain Capital Group LLC was fined $459,000, and FXCM was fined $2 million. Considering FXCM's revenue was more than $100 million per quarter, it was about the same expense as repairing a dent in the CEO's Lear jet.

Maybe the government should smarten up and fine these firms based on the percentage of their revenue instead of a maximum momentary amount. However, that will never happen because the financial lobby in Washington would fight against it tooth and nail. Robert found it amusing that his firm was using the same tools from the same technology vendor as the firms that had been fined, yet his firm had never been caught. It was not because he was smarter than those brokers; it was because they were greedy and got caught. Every broker cheats on his or her clients, but the art lies in not doing it too blatantly or too frequently.

To attract new customers, Robert's firm offered exclusive bonuses to open an FX trading account. Customers would receive a 25 percent bonus from the firm's deposit amount. For a deposit of a hundred dollars, they would receive a bonus of $25; for a $1,000 account, a bonus of $250; and for a $10,000 account, a bonus of $2,500. However, clients were not able to withdraw real money from this account until they traded a certain number of lots. To receive a $25 bonus, the holder of the $100 account had to trade three standard lots. Based on a standard two-pip spread of the EUR/USD (one pip equals $10), three standard lot trades would yield the firm $60 profit minus the $25 potential bonus. For the $10,000 account, the client would need to trade 300 lots. This would yield the firm $3,000 in spread profit minus $2,500 in potential bonuses. It was unlikely that the client would come out ahead after 300 trading lots. Many tried, but none succeeded. These bonuses were really "fake" money added to client accounts to encourage more trading. If the $10,000 client leverage was 100:1, he would have to trade an equivalent of $30 million in order to receive a meager $2,500 bonus. All beginners fell for this marketing ploy, and Robert's firm was taking the opposite trades on its clients because all these accounts were destined to get wiped out.

Robert's firm also held demo trading contests, but in that case the prizes were in real money. Any client could download the trading platform and register for a demo account to enter the competition. All participants started with $10,000 in paper money and were encouraged to obtain the highest return possible within thirty days. The client with the highest percentage gain would receive $1,500, the second $1,000, and the third $500.

Unbeknown to the participants, this was Robert's ways of recruiting new client accounts. During registration, participants submitted their names, e-mail addresses, and telephone numbers. This information was then handed over to his marketing department for sales pitches, bonus campaigns, and other third-party promotional activities.

Since it is a proven fact that most small retail traders "blow up" their accounts within three months of their first deposits, Robert's firm needed a constant supply of new customers. He achieved this by offering very low dollar account options, like the "mini" and "micro" accounts that could be opened in some cases for as little as fifty dollars. Trades from these customers would never be sent to the interbank market, but would instead be kept in his firm's inventory. At a 92 percent failure rate, the volume of these trades was pure profit to Robert's company. When one considers that the average life span of a small retail trader is about six to ten months, it is easy to see how hugely profitable this business is. The secret is in keeping a steady flow of new customers coming to a broker's door.

To vary the contests and promotional campaigns, Robert's firm would offer newly released iPhones and iPads for free, provided that the clients completed a certain number of trading lots within a thirty-day time frame. His firm rarely had to ship the free products since most traders were unable to achieve the trading lot quota in the required time.

Many traders are quite naïve to think that it is in the broker's interest to have a long-term relationship with their clients and that it is also in their interests for their clients to succeed. The argument is that as clients succeed, they will trade with larger lots and, in the process, enable the brokers to earn more on the spread. Most traders fail to succeed in trading for a living since they are unable to fathom the insurmountable challenges they are up against. Most traders think that they need to overcome only three major obstacles in trading. First is the psychology of trading, i.e., the emotional roller coaster of greed, fear, attitude, hope, despair, and regret. Overcoming these psychological roadblocks easily accounts for 70 percent of a trader's success. Second is risk management, also known as money management, which accounts for 20 percent of a trader's success. Third is the trading method or system that the trader uses, and this accounts for 10 percent of a trader's success. Unbeknown to most traders, to be successful in trading, the traders must overcome at least nine Himalaya-caliber obstacles: time, resources, discipline, money management, method, psychology, physical and mental fitness, and diversification.

Since most retail customers will fail at FX trading, it was useless for Robert's firm to develop a long-term relationship with its clients. Similar to many CEOs on Wall Street, retail FX brokers don't get rewarded for long-term plans since shareholders look only to the next quarter's results. From Robert's perspective as the sole shareholder of his firm, it was better to take whatever profit was available as quickly as possible.

Being able to operate a successful and profitable brokerage firm inevitably leads to making some enemies, so it was unavoidable that Robert's firm had disgruntled customers. It was just a matter of months when these clients started to take their complaints onto the Internet forums. Robert's firm had to hire three full-time staff members using fifteen different online nicknames to scour these forums. Their job was to post good comments and reviews about his brokerage firm. Anyone on the boards who had less-than-glowing comments about Robert's brokerage firm was immediately jumped on by these writers and made to look foolish. Robert's favorite forum staffer was known as "Billy the Bully" within the firm because he had a knack for being vicious when attacking any complainers. He was skilled at making complainers appear spineless and stupid. As his staffers were quite active on some of the forums, some of the webmasters began to take notice of them. They tracked the IP address and noticed that fifteen different nicknames were coming from the same location. Within a short time, Robert's forum staffers were banned from the forums. However, Robert knew that the dollar was king and placed advertising on these forums, and within a short period of time his staffers were back on the boards using new names. The ads provided monetary incentives for these webmasters to turn a blind eye to his staff's activities.

In order to have even more control over the forums, Robert decided to hire ten additional staffers from India to create his own forums, reviews, and content. Robert was clever enough to do this under different website domain names so that they looked like independent entities. His new FX portal sites offered free basic trading courses that explained the basics of trading and charting techniques. The newbies would be shown chart patterns and their meanings, simplistic moving average crossover trading strategies, common trading indicators, and so on. His Indian staff was active twenty-four hours a day answering any newbie trading questions. By providing as much information as possible, the neophyte FX trader would feel confident enough to open a trading account funded with his or her hard-earned money.

His firm also hired a panel of "expert analysts" from New York who would use specialized trading approaches and who followed only certain currency pairs. These so-called experts provided daily updates on post-market movements and potential trade opportunities on the firm's website, but their roles were more like Monday-morning quarterbacking. Most "experts" have very poor track records, but they are very good at presenting themselves as giving sound trading advice. They tend to dwell on their correct forecasts but sweep things under the rug quickly whenever they are wrong. In reality, this is the only way for these analysts to make a living. They are neither qualified nor good enough to trade their own money or become money managers. For them it's a great job because they risk nothing.

Robert's experts would sound intelligent and provide useful information to new traders. By providing trading ideas and intelligence updates, they offered a false sense of security that encouraged the new traders to make more trades. Nearly all new traders fail to understand that these analysts are not responsible for their followers' profits. Many new traders continue holding onto their losing trades because one of the experts made the forecast or because their analysis coincided with another expert's prediction. A newbie will tend to double up or increase his or her trading lot size when more people have agreed with his or her trade position. The market, however, does not care how many analysts have agreed with one's trading position. The market will do whatever it wants to do.

A good analogy is the human resources department of a company. Human resources personnel will go to great lengths to convince employees that the department will fight for their rights and benefits. They always say that they are on the side of the employees and that the employees can come to them with any issues or concerns. In reality, human resources staff work for the company, and it is their job to extract concerns and information from the employees and use this information against them. The broker firm analyst's job is similar to the human resources role, but the difference is that his or her job is to extract trades (money) from the clients for the benefit of the brokerage firms. Most new traders will not learn this lesson until their accounts have been blown up. Even then, they will move on to another expert, hoping for better results while repeating the same mistakes.

As for most of the broker review websites, they were either owned or sponsored by Robert's company or other FX brokers. Anyone searching for a "good" FX broker will see literally hundreds of ads and websites offering "honest and unbiased" reviews. The truth is that Robert's staff, like that of other brokerages, is hard at work giving his company raving reviews to attract new customers. It is the easiest thing in the world for brokers to hire phony "customers" who sing their praises. All the broker reviews on the Internet are easily manipulated. Anyone posting something bad about a broker will find themselves in the crosshairs of a "Billy the Bully" who will castigate and trivialize them. Most times these are not real customers but bogus people who are created by the broker-financed web writers. India is a primary source of cheap writers who work for the brokerage houses to keep the buzz surrounding a firm glowing and positive. A smart trader will need to do his or her due diligence by going to the websites of the NFA and the CTFC to see what enforcement actions may have been taken against the broker. Even then, be aware that most brokers will merely pay fines and strike a deal with these agencies that lets them off the hook by not having to plead guilty to their bad behavior. Instinctively, new traders would tend to stay away from these fined brokers. However, they may be better brokers to start a trading account with. A broker that has not been fined by the NFA is not necessarily good. The NFA has limited resources, and these brokers may not have been caught cheating and may not be under investigation—yet.

Brokers that have been fined must take drastic steps and procedures to prove to the NFA that they have changed their practices. It is unlikely that they will get caught again committing the same bad practice; however, they are more likely to use their wealth of resources to scam their clients with different schemes after things have cooled down with the NFA.

The little guy has no chance against the brokerage industry. Even if a trader can prove that he or she has been cheated by his or her broker, what can the trader do? He or she can hire a lawyer and try to sue the broker. That will take lots of time and money. For the vast majority of retail traders, this is not a realistic option. Most individuals don't have the money to hire a lawyer and go through all the stages of filing a lawsuit that could take years to conclude. One can and should file a complaint with the CTFC and the NFA, but it is a lengthy process. The trader must keep comprehensive records and provide unequivocal evidence, which may lead to the broker being fined, but, again, it is highly unlikely that the trader will ever see any money. Generally, the broker is given a slap on the wrist and then walks away to do the same bad thing, or some variation of it, to another unsuspecting victim the next day. Only big, sophisticated traders with deep pockets are likely to ever see any recompense from a broker. The deck is definitely stacked against the average retail customer. To be successful in any industry, one must be paranoid—only the ever-questioning paranoids will survive in the long run.

• • •

In addition to his trading school activities, Harry had been contacted by a representative of Robert's firm, who discussed with him the possibility of becoming an "introducing broker," or IB, for them. An IB is merely someone who acts as a portal through which a brokerage firm can get new customers from his group of followers; in Harry's case, this was his group of students. Since

Harry's school had become so successful and well known, Robert thought Harry a natural fit to help his firm add new customer accounts. All Harry had to do was steer his students to the firm, and he would receive what amounted to one pip of the standard two-pip spread per EUR/USD trade that the firm charged its customers. To Harry this was a no-brainer; of course he would recommend the firm to his students. After all, he thought all these brokers were the same (thieves dressed as respectable businessmen), and his students wouldn't be able to tell the difference anyway since they had no basis for comparison.

After graduating nearly one thousand students from his course, Harry found that almost 50 percent had taken his advice and set up accounts with Robert's brokerage company, and Harry was making one pip per round trade from each student. He couldn't believe that he was making nearly $100,000 a month for doing nothing more than acting as an introducing broker. Life didn't get much sweeter than that. Always thinking about ways to make more money, Harry came up with a brilliant idea on how to increase his IB commissions. He would sponsor trading contests among the students on a monthly basis. He would design the contests so that participants of all different income levels could compete, with no advantage being given to those who were financially better off. To do this, he would structure the contests so that the trader who made the highest percentage gain in his account that month would be the winner. In order to be eligible to compete, a trader had to be a student of Harry's school and have an account open through his IB agreement. Students would have to prove their results by sending Harry a copy of their trading account records for the entire month.

All the while, his trading contestants would be making more and more trades in an effort to try to win the prize, which would, in turn, generate more commissions to Harry from his IB agreement. It didn't really matter to him that the end result was that most of his newbie traders would be taking inappropriate risks by trading excessively in their hope of winning the contest. Harry wanted to make his prizes big enough so that his traders would be excited to participate. Being fledgling traders, they were already psychologically predisposed to overtrading and, for the most part, egotistical enough to believe they could beat the market. Harry would offer prizes of $3,000 for the trader with the highest gain, $1,500 for the second highest, and $500 for the third. This was a good starting place, Harry reckoned, and he could always adjust the prizes up or down, depending on how the contests were going. It was guaranteed that he would lose $5,000 out of $100,000 that he had been making as an IB. But he would have to see if the increase in the amount of trading would make up for his prize payouts. He could always fine-tune the amounts later if it looked like he was losing too much in prize money.

At the end of the first month's contest, Harry did have to pay out $5,000. The good news for him, however, was that he had over six hundred participants in his contest. His commissions as the IB for that month were $160,000, so he netted a profit of $155,000. Harry was over the moon. He resisted the temptation to increase the prize money to attract more participants, and he wanted to see if this first month might have just been a fluke.

At the end of the second month, Harry saw the fruits of his labors grow amazingly. He kept the total prize money payout at $5,000, but his commissions that month from the brokerage came in at a staggering $240,000. Harry was on fire. Why hadn't he thought about this sooner? Life didn't get better than this—he had stumbled upon a veritable money-making machine.

SUMMARY OF CHAPTER 6

1. Priority is given to the bigger clients.

Larger accounts of $25,000 or more are treated much more fairly and will be put on a different computer server because FX brokers do not want to keep big trades in-house and face the risk of them going against the house. Consequently, they will send them to the interbank market for a legitimate counterparty to trade. This gives the large account trader a huge advantage over the little retail trader.

2. Small-account FX traders are a broker's cash cow.

Most retail FX brokers inventory the small account customers, defined as those with accounts of less than $5,000. For these customers, different trading servers and operating procedures are put in place. These are the customers that make the real money for the FX broker. Through various unethical practices such as stop tripping, price shading, re-quoting, etc., the odds are always stacked in the broker's favor, and the little retail trader has very little likelihood of ever coming out ahead.

3. Different servers from the same broker will affect systematic trading results.

Even with identical trading software running, different servers from the same broker will affect trading results. The brokers can wreak havoc on systematic trading software by providing inconsistent price feeds. This problem is further exacerbated when trading via the same software with different FX brokers. In the world of systematic trading, this is known as "GIGO"—garbage in, garbage out.

4. Brokerage firms will go to great lengths to discredit the "92 percent lose" statistic.

Brokerage firms have too much to lose, and they will generate lots of misinformation and disinformation to confuse retail traders. They may also try to discredit this book and its author.

5. Most customer complaints never ripen into lawsuits.

A small retail trader with a $500 or a $5,000 account taken by a broker's shenanigans would likely never recover his or her money. The trader would spend much more pursuing a lawsuit than he or she could hope to receive even if he or she did win the case. The brokerage houses all know this and have teams of expensive lawyers on retainer to protect them from such lawsuits. When opening your FX trading account, don't let your broker use your information—trading experience, annual income, liquid assets, etc.—to trade against you.

6. **If you do proceed with arbitration or legal action, detailed record keeping is essential.**

Without records of trades and timing, the judge or arbitrator has no basis for a decision.

7. **Retail traders are most often poorly served by trading books and trading instructors.**

Trading books or trading instructors will rarely reveal that there are at least ten different ways your broker can work against you. The authors of most trading books want only to inspire you to stay in the game; what they won't tell you is why the game is so difficult in the first place.

8. **Most "expert analysts" have very poor trading records.**

They tend to dwell upon their correct forecasts and quickly sweep their missteps under the rug. The analysts' job is to extract trades and money from the clients to benefit the brokerage firm. They are very good at presenting themselves as giving sound trading advice, all the while risking nothing.

CHAPTER 7

THE DEVIL IS IN THE DETAILS

Ron had become addicted to the market. Much like a gambler, he found that he could not stay away from the FX market for longer than the time he was asleep at night. Even then, sometimes he woke up in the middle of the night and would check the tail end of the Asian session and the beginning of the London session. But Ron's favorite trading time was between 8:00 a.m. and noon New York time, when the vast majority of FX trading activity took place and trade volume hit its daily peak. This was also the period when the markets were the most volatile, and Ron thrived on this unpredictability.

Ron's trading addiction had reached the point that he hated to see the weekend come. Unlike the vast majority of people who look forward to their weekend rest and recreation, Ron couldn't wait for the new trading week to begin. His McDonald's franchises mostly ran themselves at this point. He had been very wise in his selection of store managers and the regional managers above them. He found that he needed to meet with his regional managers only once a week, on Monday afternoons after two (to make sure that he wasn't missing any good trading opportunities) via teleconference from his home office. The rest of his week was left open for his trading habit.

Like any good junkie, Ron facilitated his habit. He had monitors strategically placed all over his mansion, even in his bathrooms, so that with the push of a remote control (which he carried with him at all times) he could see exactly what was happening in the market. His wife smirked each time she walked by him. Ron had made a makeshift remote-control holster on the right side of his belt. She felt like she was in a western movie where there was a sheriff ready to spring to her rescue at a moment's notice, albeit with only his remote control in hand. Ron had apps galore on his iPhone that would bring up FX analytic services, from fundamental analysis to technical analysis and everything in between. When he left the house for any reason, he made sure he was connected to the market via his iPhone. He had even installed a satellite TV system in his car so he could pull up any FX price chart while he was driving. This was a dangerous distraction, but Ron didn't care.

What Ron did not realize was that too much information created more excitement and more anxiety for him. Whenever the news or market analysts agreed with his predictions on the market, it caused him to become highly excited. Unfortunately, whenever Ron was excited, he was prone to making poor trading decisions, such as increasing his bet size per trade. It seemed that his "sure bets" were always his biggest losers. Whenever the experts disagreed with Ron's market predictions, his anxiety shot through the roof. This anxiety would cause him to doubt himself, and he would exit his winning trades too early. He became addicted to market information from all sources, which he hoped would make him a better trader. But his trading results got worse. He was attempting to become a "techno-fundamentalist," where he was mixing technical and fundamental techniques. Being ill-informed, Ron did not realize that he had to master one method first before attempting to combine it with any others. Fundamental trading was for long-term position trades that would take weeks or months to play out, while technical trading would happen within minutes or hours. The majority of the time technical trading would conflict with Ron's fundamental understanding of the market, and this created further confusion for him.

Ron loved the rush the market gave him. He loved the whole process of taking in information on the market from as many sources as possible and then synthesizing it to come up with a trading plan. This input was an amalgam of expert research based on both fundamental and technical analyses. The act of evaluating all this information made him feel like he was a real player, a professional FX trader equal to the big boys on Wall Street. He hated the fact that his body actually needed to sleep at least six hours a day. What a waste of time, Ron thought. Maybe he could hire some trading assistants to watch over his trades while he was asleep; that way he could be in the market twenty-four hours a day. Alternatively, Ron had been doing some research on the use of trading "robots," or automated systematic computer programs that would make trades using preprogrammed criteria. If he could get one that really worked, he could just monitor its daily progress and never miss a good trading opportunity. It would be like printing money.

When his trades were going in the right direction and Ron was "in the money," there was not a happier person on earth.

However, when the market went against him, Ron became uncontrollably angry and depressed. He found it very difficult to cut his losses by exiting a losing trade. Early in his trading experience, he had a nearly disastrous experience of letting a trade run two hundred pips against his position and riding with it until the market reversed. Fortunately, it not only made up the two hundred-pip loss, but went forty pips in Ron's favor, at which time he closed his trade with a profit. Ron knew this experience went against what most trading experts taught, including Harry from his trading-school course, but Ron figured he was smarter than the so-called experts. After all, how many of them had taken themselves from nothing to becoming a multimillionaire by building a mega-successful business?

Most trading gurus teach that you should never risk more than 1 percent of your capital on a single trade. Since Ron was a multimillionaire, he could always add more capital to his trading account if he had to, so he thought the 1 percent rule didn't apply to him. Unwittingly, this lack of financial discipline was digging him into a bigger and bigger hole. Since he had so much money available to him to play the market, he made bad trade selections, and the market began to play with him in a big way. Limited funds to the average trader, especially professional traders, cause them to trade conservatively. It was a natural brake on impulsive trading behavior. With seemingly unlimited resources, Ron didn't have this concern and became more and more reckless in his trading. As a consequence, he was beginning to take some significant losses. This was starting to scare his wife, who brought his trading obsession to his attention more than once. In fact, Ron's wife saw his behavior as a gambling addiction. Many say that trading is essentially a sophisticated form of gambling. It provides all the thrills and chills of a poker table or roulette wheel. With each trade, there is the possibility of winning or losing. The thrill is in the not knowing which way the trade will go. But professional gamblers follow the same advice as professional traders; they set limits to the amount they are willing to lose on any given hand. Over the long run, this discipline will keep them out of the weeds and in positive territory. The addict gambler, like the addict trader, will be willing to go for broke literally on a single hand.

A typical week for Ron would look something like this: Sunday evening, around 11:00 p.m. New York time, he would check his charts to see what was happening in the Asian session. He would take notes about what he saw and how he thought his favorite currency pair, the EUR/USD, was acting. He realized that the Asian session was typically a slow session and that things really began to heat up once London came online at 3:00 a.m. New York time. The euro was presenting Ron with wonderful opportunities due to its trading volatility caused by the European debt crisis. Every week it seemed that another member country was about to withdraw from the European Union, which caused the euro to lose value as FX traders sought the security of "risk assets"—i.e., stable currencies such as the dollar, which was weak against the euro, but politically safe. However, whenever any bad economic news came out in the United States, the euro would climb in value again as confidence in the dollar would decline.

On this particular Sunday, the news from Sydney was grim. Earnings reports were due out on Monday for many of the largest US multinational corporations, and the analysts were predicting that most of them would fall short of their earnings projections. This news was depressing the dollar in Asian trading. Ron checked all of his FX subscription newsletters and services (he had twenty-four), and from this, he saw a consensus of opinion that indicated the dollar would fall further in early Monday trading. After following the market for two hours, at 9:25 p.m., Ron bought 200 standard lots of the EUR/USD at 1.3050. Ron's broker provided the statutory maximum leverage of 1:50, which meant that he had to have a margin in $400,000, or 40 percent of his $1 million account was locked up. This also meant that every pip movement equaled $2,000. Ron was certain that it was a sure win; hence, he was swinging for the fences. This was truly the indication that Ron was a gambler masquerading as a trading addict. A gambler would always focus on the potential winning possibilities, unlike a good trader who would always focus on his potential loss per trade. Fortunately for him, his wife knew almost nothing about his trading account or his trading activity, other than being able to tell if he had won or lost by the elation or anger he exhibited.

Ron had found over time that he was really interested in trading only the EUR/USD since it accounted for over 30 percent of the volume of the FX spot market. Most trading experts recommended to him to concentrate on one or two pairs so that he could develop a feel for them, which made it somewhat easier to anticipate their next movements. He didn't know why, but Ron just felt more comfortable with this pair. He had traded the Cable, the Yen, the Swissy, EUR/JPY, and GBP/JPY, but he always came back to the EUR/USD.

On Monday morning, Ron woke up to find that the EUR/USD had been trading higher in the London session and was now up fifty pips, meaning that Ron was ahead by $100,000. By the close of the New York session, the euro was up against the dollar by 120 pips, and Ron had made a floating profit of $240,000. Not bad for one day's work, he thought. He decided to let his trade "ride" overnight because the consensus opinion from all of his technical and fundamental sources was that the euro was going higher again against the dollar in the next few weeks.

On Tuesday, the euro rose another eighty pips against the dollar when more news came out that the US economy had a drop in retail sales for the prior month. As a result, Ron's account increased by another $400,000. He was overjoyed, so overjoyed that he bought his wife a new diamond bracelet that cost $125,000.

But on Wednesday, as it inevitably happens, profit taking started. The EUR/USD plunged by seventy-five pips, costing Ron $150,000. This still left him with an overall net profit of $250,000. Once more, checking all of his information sources, he believed that the euro was still heading higher, as he knew from experience to expect profit taking after a currency pair ran in one direction for several sessions. He viewed the euro's current direction as a temporary "correction" that would turn around and head back up against the dollar within a day or two.

On Thursday, good economic news was coming out of the European Union, where the EU Central Bank announced that it was providing additional loans to two of its member countries that were in severe financial distress. This news was supposed to be good because it temporarily allayed fears of a total meltdown of the euro. Unfortunately, the bottom fell out of the euro, and it was down by 150 pips. It did not make any sense to Ron why the euro went down on good news. Many of the experts on TV were touting buy on the rumors and sell on the facts. By Thursday night, the euro dropped another seventy-five pips, which evaporated his $400,000 floating profit, and Ron was in the red for $200,000. Unable to further sustain the emotional roller-coaster ride and the volatility of the market, Ron got out with a loss of $200,000.

On Friday morning, the euro rallied a hundred pips and ended flat for the entire trading week. Ron was fuming. If only he had stayed with his trade for just one more day, he could have avoided losing $200,000—more than most Americans earned in one year. On top of that, Ron had to foot the bill for the $125,000 diamond bracelet that he did not want to return because of his pride. He then understood why so many Americans got their homes repossessed during financial crises. Like many Americans, Ron counted his chickens before the eggs hatched.

Ron was infuriated since all of his financial advisory subscriptions were actually correct. The majority of the subscriptions were bullish, and the euro did rise during the beginning of the week. Some of his subscriptions were bearish, and the euro did collapse during the middle of the week. A few of his subscriptions were dovish on the euro, and they were also correct because the euro ended flat by the end of the week. Ron squeezed his head hard with both of his palms, hoping to compress all the brain matter in his skull. He was trying to figure out the solution to this convoluted trading game. If each of his advisory services was correct, why didn't he make any money? Was it possible to lose money when everyone was correct? Ron understood that his emotions and lack of discipline played a big role in his losses, but there was a fundamental hidden truth that he had yet to substantiate and solidify.

Then it dawned upon Ron that he was just like those infant baboons he had seen as a child at the zoo. With all its unpredictability and chaos, the market was just like a jungle. But the jungle does not just have bulls and bears—there are also baboons. What he was starting to realize was that in the financial industry, the marketers and promoters were the rulers, a.k.a. the "super baboons." These multinational media conglomerates created the bull and bear to entertain their vast audience. Whenever, the market moved up by 0.01 percent or more, they would promote the bull as if the prices were going to shoot to the moon tomorrow. Whenever prices dropped by 0.01 percent or more, the bear was in charge, and the end of the world was coming. They oversimplified the market into the bull and bear to water down the information so that it could be easily by swallowed by the naïve traders. These super baboons made their living by grabbing sensational headlines to make mountains out of molehills solely to entertain their viewers.

Then there were the "regular baboons," such as the advisory services and trainers like Harry, whose primary job was to make themselves look smart and credible. By marketing themselves as intellectuals and independent thinkers, they would always be perceived as correct and infallible in their forecasts, regardless of the actual market direction. They would conveniently leave out the crucial fact that the FX market does not just move up and down; it is a juggernaut because it also moves sideways and in haphazard directions. Whether these regular baboons are aware of this and are deliberately overlooking it to make FX trading more marketable, or whether they are simply ignorant of this fact—and this should not be a surprise since their expertise is often unfounded—is not really the issue, seeing that their ploy seems to work perfectly all the time.

The average trader is the "infant baboon" in this animal kingdom, and that's basically what Ron felt like he was. Just like most novice traders, he would helplessly succumb to their hypnoses and find himself behaving like a puppet in a puppet show orchestrated by those superior baboons. The "monkey say, monkey do" cliché was effortlessly brought to life with novice traders, and this fact was hugely unsettling for Ron. He felt shame and belittlement that they had unashamedly manipulated him and others like him and realized that he needed to act now.

Expectedly, the super baboons and regular baboons did not guarantee profit for their followers. Ron did not care much for discerning the signals from the market noises anymore. He just wanted to be successful in trading. He changed his strategy to real-time market signal services. Many of these signal services transmitted the exact timing of entry and exit of each trade. With this exact timing, the results were more concrete, reproducible, and were not open to interpretation as they were with the advisory services. Before he could take that step, Ron had to confess to his wife about his recent loss. What he didn't share was his $3.1 million in losses during the past six months.

At long last, he had a heart-to-heart talk with his wife. He told her what she had already been observing anyway, that he was addicted to trading, blindly following the information on his trading subscription services as well as all the books and online FX trading sources on a daily basis. None of it worked. In fact, it just clouded his judgment and impaired his trading abilities. She told him that if he still wanted to trade, she would support him, but he should also seek to balance his work life with other parts of his life so that he could achieve a better mental state. She suggested that he get back into the daily meditation routine he originally practiced before he started trading. He fell away from all of his daily stress-reduction practices as his obsession with trading and following FX news and information became more extreme.

One of the many things Ron loved about his wife was her clear-headedness. She always seemed to know what was wrong with him and how to fix it. What a lucky man I am to have such a woman, he said to himself. He stopped trading altogether, but he didn't close his trading account—he just let it sit dormant.

He needed a breather and time to get his head straight. Looking back on the last year, he saw how all the information and opinions from so many sources had conspired to give him information overload. Instead of making him a better trader, all it did was make him more egotistical and reckless.

Ron also made it a ritual to meditate fifteen minutes every morning. He had been advised that he should meditate for at least forty-five minutes per session twice a day, but he just couldn't, try as he might. It seemed that Ron always knew a significant amount of effort was required to obtain the optimum results; however, he was constantly looking for ways to cut corners. He was similar to many people who constantly look for shortcuts in life—those who try to learn a language in ten days, lose twenty pounds in two weeks, get flat abs in five minutes, or gain financial freedom with FX trading in just thirty minutes a day. The marketers were able to create attention-grabbing headlines for the unsuspecting consumers, creating a culture in which consumers expected maximum results with minimum effort on their part.

FX traders can experience high levels of stress while they trade. They are focused on increasing profits, preventing loss, all the while keeping up with both technical and fundamental trading techniques, updates, and information. This information overload causes a great deal of stress that can unbalance a trader. Meditating can help get traders back in the "optimum zone," provided they put in a significant amount of time and effort. Practicing meditation helps a trader to center himself or herself, allowing him or her to become more aware of the present moment, which eventually leads to growth. Proper breathing awareness decreases heart rate, allowing breathing to become more controlled. Together, these allow the trader to become sharper and more balanced. The more focused a trader is, the better he or she will able to control his or her emotions and avoid making trade decisions based on fear and greed—the two enemies of trading success. A relaxed trader is a balanced trader who looks for ways to prevent trading mistakes instead of swinging for the fence. Trading in the optimum zone is when trading feels natural—without stress or concern about profits. When a trader is balanced, there is neither the paralyzing emotion of fear nor the elation of the gambling rush. Proper meditation allows a balanced trader to focus better and to direct negative energy away, so he or she can trade with confidence.

• • •

Cynthia was at her wit's end. Her mathematically sound trading formula had not worked out the way she had predicted. She had set a goal of increasing her trading account by 5 percent a day, based on making a hundred dollars a day for twenty trading days a month. Making a hundred dollars a day on her $2,000 trading account seemed to her to be easy to achieve—she even allowed for two or three days of losses per month. She would trade using a lot size that would produce a ten-dollar pip. All she had to do was make ten pips a day to reach her goal of a $100 profit per day. That seemed to her to be very easy to do. Through the magic of compounding, she projected that by the end of her seventh month of trading, she would make $178,000.

However, the market had other ideas, and Cynthia's plan did not work out very well. Within nine months, she had lost three $2,000 accounts. Cynthia was by nature an extremely competitive person, and she had chosen the real-estate business because her aggressiveness and perseverance were well suited to that field. She was the type of person who rarely took no for an answer.

It infuriated her that her FX trading wasn't going according to plan. FX was supposed to be her ace in the hole, her path to financial independence.

Once again, Cynthia reloaded her trading account with another $2,000. This was the fourth time she had done so. She was determined to get back at the market and make it pay. This emotionality caused her to override, and within a month of investing more money in her account, she had blown through it. She had been placing bigger bets by using larger lot sizes, hoping to make back her losses more quickly. In reality, all she was doing was accelerating her downward spiral.

The ironic thing about Cynthia was that when she started in the real-estate business, it was uncertain that she could sell twenty-four houses per year. There were fast months in which she sold four houses. There were slow months in which she sold one or none. Her monthly average was two houses, but there was no guarantee that she would sell two houses a month consistently. Cynthia had to budget her spending accordingly. She saved up during her good months so that she could ride out the bad months and still cover her monthly expenses. Somehow, this averaging did not apply to FX trading. There was an expectation of upward mobility that she could constantly earn ten pips a day and then compound her constant daily profits to achieve financial nirvana. Let's assume that ten pips per day was possible. Why should a trader stop there? Why wouldn't he or she set a target of ten pips for every four hours or ten pips every hour? Given that there is a constant fluctuation in the currency market, there were bound to be movements of twenty to thirty pips each hour on at least one of the many currency pairs.

It is great to set goals. However, setting daily trading goals and expecting to achieve them is a fool's errand. It will not happen because the FX market is not a beast you can tame and control or bend to your will. Instead, it will bend you to its will. The best you can do is play the averages and try to set long-term goals. There are just too many variations in the day-to-day moves of the market. Day-to-day market variation is particularly attractive to those traders who trade using shorter time-frame charts. These short-time-frame traders are also known as scalpers. On average, they hold trades for less than four hours. They do not let their winning trades turn into losing trades and quickly exit their trade at any sign of a market reversal. As a result, scalpers have high winning trade percentages. Unfortunately, they are also known to hold large losing trade positions when they are wrong. Sometimes, in order to achieve a winning trade, they may hold a losing trade of two hundred pips or more until the trade reverses in their favor by a few pips. One losing trade of a scalper can wipe out the total profits of twenty previous winning trades.

Cynthia had thought that the best way for her to reach her daily goal was to play the shorter time frames, and, accordingly, she had settled down to the one minute, the fifteen minutes, and the thirty minute charts because she couldn't stand waiting to see how her trade was moving in the longer time-frame charts. For some reason, she thought she would be able to win more pips by playing the shorter movements of these charts. Instead, what happened was that she was constantly getting whipsawed because she was constantly pushing trades to meet her quota. Couple this with her propensity to overtrade, and the combination was lethal.

Cynthia did not understand the requirements to create a positive expectancy for her trading system. She neglected to understand the reward-risk ratio and how a certain winning percentage was required to average ten pips a day. To her, it wasn't about achieving the average ten pips per day, but a fixed and constant net profit of ten pips each day. In reality, any daily goal is delusional since trading is not a production line where you can automatically produce a fixed result each hour or each day. A trader can take only what the market gives him. Some days a trader is handsomely rewarded, and some days a trader may be badly beaten by the market. A production line can only produce a constant expected output if the input and process is constant. Unfortunately, the market is the input, and it is not constant. An expectation of constant output with a varying input is wishful thinking.

Cynthia had become as addicted to the FX market as Ron. She read everything she could get her hands on relating to trading. She particularly liked reading profile articles on "superstar" fund managers. She loved their success stories and how they became millionaires, even billionaires in some cases, starting with little or nothing but their burning desire to succeed. That was Cynthia all over. Ever since she was a little girl growing up in East Los Angeles in what some would refer to as the *barrio*, she had told herself she would succeed and overcome the poverty of her childhood. At school, she always got top grades and won a full scholarship to UC Berkeley, where she earned her undergraduate degree in business administration and graduated magna cum laude.

Reading stories and profiles of famous and successful people, especially traders, can lead most people into believing that they too can duplicate their success. The truth is that they can't. If this were true, there would be a thousand times more superstars. The reason people don't achieve the same results is mostly because they don't put in the same amount of effort over the same period of time with the same level of persistence. The long, hard struggle of these successful people is generally glossed over, and their many failures before finally reaching success are never mentioned. Most people want to be inspired by the success of others. Unfortunately, very few have the dedication, work ethic, and willingness to make the sacrifices necessary to achieve greatness. The reality is that for every trading superstar, there are a thousand struggling traders with broken marriages and bankruptcies.

Some trading gurus say that becoming a great FX trader is like becoming a doctor; it takes years of practice, a hefty tuition fee, and hard work. But the reality is quite different. In order to get into medical school, one has to take the Medical College Admissions Test and do very well on it. In addition, the candidate for medical school must come from a good college or university where he or she has done very well academically and achieved an almost perfect GPA. He or she will also need to show that he or she is "well rounded" by having extracurricular activities on his or her résumé. Admissions to medical school are highly self-selecting, unlike becoming an FX trader, where the only requirement is the amount of money needed to open a trading account or pay trading-course tuition. Harry knew this when he opened his trading school, but he took advantage of the basic human instinct in everyone that they too could achieve success with the right tools and training. Harry knew that he could make a lot of money providing inspiration to his students, even though he was unqualified to provide the proper training. Since most people are gung-ho on getting rich quick, Harry knew that he had found his gold mine in FX training.

Cynthia, by nature and nurture, was not a girl to take rejection lying down. But the FX market was rejecting her. Much like her experience with would-be lovers, where their rejection increased her desire and ambition to win their love, she bristled at her losses in the market and became even more determined to win. She continued to read and try to teach herself new systems and theories on how to win in the FX market. The "experts" and her celebrity traders said never to make emotional trades. Cynthia was smart enough to recognize that this was a major personality flaw of hers and that it was leading to her failure as an FX trader. Like Ron, she was addicted to the market and followed it constantly throughout the day. She too wished that she could somehow follow the action 24/7.

This got her to thinking about the benefits of using a trading robot. A robot could provide help to her in a number of ways. First, it would not be emotional. It would make only the trades that it was programmed to make, nothing more and nothing less. Second, it would watch the market twenty-four hours a day so that it would be able to take advantage of developing trade setups while she was asleep or doing other things.

Cynthia started to notice the bags under her eyes. She was getting only four to five hours of sleep a night. With each passing day, she became more convinced that FX trading was an impossible way to make money. Conscious of her deteriorating appearance and lack of success in FX, she started having reservations about trading. Then one day, one of her clients told her about his success in investing in gold. Cynthia became increasingly curious about gold investing. Unlike FX trading, gold investing seemed much more of a sure thing. And so, it wasn't long before Cynthia closed her currency trading account and opened a gold brokerage account. FX had become just the latest casualty in her never-ending quest to achieve financial independence.

• • •

Charlie had been trying to figure out how to make money at FX for the five years since he had taken Harry's course. He remembered how Harry made it seem inevitable that any serious person who learned the trading techniques could trade his or her way to limitless wealth. Charlie had turned his $2,000 into $30,000 in thirty days, but the market, as Charlie was to learn, was a cruel mistress, and she took all of his profits back and the rest of his trading account as well. The "law of large numbers" had caught up with him—it was easy to obtain a large profit quickly, but it was impossible to sustain his trading results.

Charlie couldn't stay away from the market, and, like an addict, he was hooked on it. After blowing up his $30,000 winning account, he decided to get back at the market and put another $10,000 into his account. He believed that since he was successful once, he could repeat his success. Within four weeks he had blown through that money as well. Now, infuriated with himself and the market, Charlie took another $10,000 from his savings account and put it into his trading account. Trying to be more conservative in his trading, Charlie limited himself to taking no more than four trades a week. He thought that the reason for his prior losses was due to overtrading, and, in all fairness, it was, at least in part.

Within a few months, Charlie was back to a zero balance in his trading account. This pattern repeated itself over a two-year period. Charlie eventually lost his entire life savings of $130,000. Early in his trading, he was spending only two hours a day looking at the charts and two hours perusing the forums and other websites for ideas. Later he was spending fifteen hours a day on FX activities. He had become obsessed with watching and trading the market, looking for possible setups on all time frames. He had a bloodlust for the market and vowed that he would defeat it. He had given up all of his other interests, such as cooking and watching movies. Charlie did not realize that spending fifteen hours a day on FX would not make him richer or a better trader. In fact, the more time he spent looking at charts and FX news, the more he was being counterproductive. These extra long hours did not count toward the ten thousand hours of useful training. Trading is unlike a production line, where the longer you run the line, the more output it produces. Sometime a trader can place forty trades over a period of two months, and his or her net result will be zero, or worse, a loss. Other times, a trader can place four good trades, and they will produce all of his or her profits.

Most trend traders have problems during sideways markets, and most sideways traders have problems with trending markets. A sideways market can be as long as several months, and the more effort a trend trader makes will not necessarily yield more profitable results. Trading is more than being in the right place at the right time. Traders must take the appropriate actions to generate profits or to defend against losses. They also have to be at their optimum mental capacity at all times when they are trading. Most traders would get disheartened if they didn't find any trading opportunities during a given week, whereas a disciplined trader would stick to one single currency pair without any wavering for several weeks.

In many respects, trading is similar to fishing. A fisherman must study tides and currents and their effects on the fish. A newbie can waste hours casting and trolling when the tide is wrong, whereas a fisherman who knows tides would pick only the most favorable fishing periods. A newbie fisherman would get extremely enthusiastic about learning how to fish. He would try to learn as much and as quickly as possible, but he would still be unsuccessful. The devil is in the details because a new fisherman still needs to learn about what lines and bait to use. Depending on the type of fish he is trying to catch, he may need longer and more sensitive poles with different baits. Some days he won't catch anything, but some days he won't miss. Trading requires a lot of patience, and so does fishing. Unlike patience in fishing, which can be counted in hours and days, patience in trading can be counted in weeks and months. Unfortunately, most traders don't have this type of patience. Some new traders get lucky after a few months or several years, but the real traders are the ones who are still successful after a decade or more.

Strangely, Charlie found himself thinking more and more about Harry and his FX course. He checked, and it appeared that Harry was still offering the course. What Charlie had come to discover since then was that all the information Harry was charging a lot of money for was readily available online and given away free by the various brokerage houses. Some websites were offering free online courses and had more information than Harry did in his course. As Charlie researched the Internet, he found numerous offerings for one-on-one trading coach services and trading psychology classes.

Trying to fight his way out of the rut, Charlie took out a line of credit on his house to sign up for more training courses and to fund his trading addiction. One coach was teaching the trading secrets to retiring in five years with just $10,000 in trading capital. He advertised that there was nothing to lose and touted the possibility to generate a six-figure income for retirement. Another course was on identifying various market conditions and how to trade them. One coach claimed that he could make ten pips per day, and he could do it all day long. Another coach was claiming to trade his own money with every trading signal from his proprietary trading system with a 99 percent winning trade record. Charlie got suckered into yet another trading course when a new trader claimed to make $7,000 in three days by taking a course from a ten-year veteran trader of a billion-dollar hedge fund.

Regardless of how many courses he took, none of them delivered on what was promised. It seemed that each course was competing against the others and delivered over-the-top promises without any substance to back them up. All of these trainers and coaches were skilled at marketing and excellent at analyzing what had happened in the market. However, none had actually opened their trading account statements to show their trading results or had their trading results validated by a third party. Most of these so-called experts fabricated discussions of economic fundamentals during their live trading sessions. However, none of them demonstrated long-term profitable trading results after six months. A few shared trading records of less than a year and with fewer than a hundred trades.

Charlie was disgusted by all the lies. He wished that he was articulate and a good presenter so he could market himself as a trading guru, since he was able to turn $2,000 into $30,000 within one month. It was unfortunate that he was an introvert and unable to express himself. He believed that all these scoundrels should go to jail for what they were selling. Unfortunately, all these marketers also had an army of lawyers to protect them. There were no legal claims or promises being offered, and they all placed disclaimers in their ads that "past performance does not guarantee future success." This was sufficient to keep them from being liable to their customers for any losses they might incur. Being human, most people ignored these disclaimers and focused instead on the potential profits that these marketers claimed could be made using their systems or information. They appealed to the greed of these would-be traders to expose their wallets for easy picking.

Charlie began to have frightful nightmares. In his recurring bad dreams, he locked up several of his FX coaching mentors in his basement. He would conduct experiments on them, whereby he would provide his trainers with news releases about the market. He would then require each of them to predict whether the market would go up or down. When one got it wrong, Charlie would administer an electric shock until foam started to come out of that person's mouth. All of his mentors picked either up or down markets, and all got shocked when the market moved sideways. His most terrible nightmare was when he saw a vision of the mentor who claimed that he could produce several profitable trades of ten pips per day. In this type of dream, Charlie would saw off the mentor's finger with a hacksaw for each day that the mentor failed to deliver his daily quota. Charlie was waking up in the middle of the night in cold sweats with lingering, gruesome images of his nightmares.

The more Charlie lost money trading, the more he thought about Harry, and the more negative his view of him became. Harry had made it seem that anyone with half a brain could win at FX if he or she only followed his training advice. Charlie had tried out all of Harry's techniques and systems and had been disciplined (or so he thought) with it, and still he had lost over $250,000 to the market. Was Harry to blame since Harry first introduced Charlie to FX trading? Was it Harry's pitch that everyone could trade for a living? Was it the fact that Harry, while not blatantly lying to his students, came so close to lie territory that he was guilty of misleading them about their chances of FX trading success? Had he told them, or had he insinuated that they would become rich trading FX? The more he thought about it, the more Charlie became angry at Harry for luring him and others into the FX black hole.

Charlie had communicated with some of his gang of seven classmates, who told him what their experience with FX had been since taking Harry's class, and many seemed to be suffering from the same FX addiction. This made Charlie certain that Harry was the villain in this plot. How many more people would Harry harm by sucking them into the FX trap? How many more savings accounts would be emptied because of Harry's sales pitch or others like him? Charlie thought something should be done; Harry was a menace to society and would continue to hurt more people unless he was stopped. But what could Charlie do? Technically, he knew that Harry had not broken any laws, except perhaps moral laws. He would never be arrested and put away, which is what Charlie thought should happen. It was wrong that Harry could continue his vile business. Someone had to do something about it, but who could do it? Charlie? If not Charlie, then who? Charlie's enmity toward Harry grew by the day, and he found that he could not shake it, no matter how hard he tried.

By now Charlie had become almost a complete recluse. He rarely left the house, and when he did, it was just to run errands, never for anything social or fun. Like an alcoholic or drug addict, Charlie could not leave his lover "Madame FX" for very long. He would actually get nervous and irritable if he couldn't see what the market was doing. The only time he got any rest was on the weekends when the market was closed. But this was a double-edged sword because he suffered withdrawal symptoms from not being able to see the market in action. Deep in his bones, Charlie knew something was wrong with him mentally; he just didn't know what it was or what to do about it.

SUMMARY OF CHAPTER 7

1. Too much information hinders trading.

By diligently following countless analysts, expert opinions, and FX information sources, a trader will be doing himself more harm than good. The constant striving for more information in the attempt to perfect one's trading strategy can cause the trader to become a "techno-fundamentalist," mixing technical and fundamental techniques together. Fundamental trading is for long-term position trades, which take weeks or months to play out, while technical trading happens within a few minutes or hours. The majority of the time, technical trading conflicts with fundamental analyses of the market, providing the trader with convoluted and impractical information that does nothing but debilitate trading and further compound losses.

2. FX trading can evolve into another form of gambling.

The fact that the currency market operates around the clock can prompt the trader to constantly monitor and eventually have his or her life wholly centered on the market. The way that a gambler becomes addicted to gambling, an FX trader may become addicted to FX trading and even exhibit the same habits. A gambler will always focus on the potential winning possibilities; however, a good trader will always focus on his or her potential loss per trade.

3. It is unrealistic to have consistent output with varying input.

A constant output is possible only if the input and the process is constant. Unfortunately, the market is the input, and it is nowhere near constant. Setting daily trading goals and expecting to achieve them is a fool's errand. Assuming that ten pips per day is possible, why not set set the target at every four hours or every hour? FX trading is not like a production line where a set of inputs yield an expected set of outputs. It has a wholly different dynamic that plays out on its own terms.

4. Currency markets are unpredictable as a rule.

Expert opinions of market movements are generally based upon hindsight and could not be applied in real time to generate consistant profits. Innate volatility—as well as economic, political, and social variables that influence the market—make prediction impossible.

5. Discipline is the key to profitability.

The volatility of the currency market is unparalleled, and the market cannot be monitored manually by the average individual. Profits can quickly evaporate into losses within hours, and a disciplined strategy that cuts losses short and lets profits run is crucial to offset this volatility. It is simply impossible for a trader to make long-term, consistent trading decisions based on observing the market and its constant fluctuations and manually execute trades.

6. FX experts rarely provide additional insight.

FX experts conjure up the bull and bear to entertain their audiences. Whenever the market moves up by 0.01 percent or more, they promote the bull, as if prices are going to shoot to the moon tomorrow. Whenever prices drop by 0.01 percent or more, the bear is in charge, and the end of the world is coming. They make their living by grabbing sensational headlines, making mountains out of molehills solely to entertain their viewers. The green trader more often than not falls victim to these invalid opinions that are framed as if they were revelations.

7. It is important to have a balanced life through meditation.

Practicing meditation helps a trader with stress reduction; however, it must be done for at least forty-five minutes per session. Meditation helps center a trader to become more aware of his or her breathing and of the present moment. This centering will allow the trader to have better control of his or her emotions. A balanced trader does not exude jubilation when the trade is going in his or her favor nor is he or she angry or depressed when a trade is going against him or her.

8. The financial market contains the bull, the bear, and the baboon.

The jungle market is being oversimplified into the bulls and the bears; however, there are also the baboons. New traders must understand that most of the services available are to entertain and to inform; however, these services are not responsible for the new traders' profitability. In order to ensure profitability, the service must provide the exact price and timing of the entries and exits. This will ensure that the results are replicatable.

CHAPTER 8

A THOUSAND LIVE TRADES TO DISCOVER THE TRADING EDGE

Jane stopped trading. She sought refuge in trading to get her out of her personal problems, but the reality of the trading world hit her like a concrete slab. She and her husband, Peter, had been trying to have a child for nearly five years with no luck. During that time, they had spent a small fortune on various fertility procedures, but nothing seemed to help. They finally came to the conclusion that they would never be able to have their own child. This was one of the reasons that Jane started trading in the first place; for her, it was a way to change the subject, getting her mind off not being able to have a child. But recently Peter, for the first time, had suggested that they look into adopting, and she was finally willing to consider this possibility.

The reason Peter was now on board with adoption was to regain the intimacy in their relationship that had been lacking for quite some time. Peter felt Jane drifting further and further away from him, in part because of her obsession with trading. He knew that it was a way for her to shift focus from the lack of children. By compulsively immersing herself in all aspects of FX trading, she effectively removed herself from that reality. Nevertheless, it came with a price, and Peter was very fearful that if things continued on the way they were, their relationship would not survive. Above all else, Peter loved his wife, and the thought of divorce was unthinkable to him, so he was the one to push for adoption, thinking that a child would cement their relationship and distract Jane from her trading addiction.

It was the baby talk that moved Jane away from trading; she had temporarily stopped trading because she was suffering from "trader's burnout." She had spent the last five years learning everything she could about FX trading, beginning with taking Harry's course to reading every book on the subject she could get her hands on. Additionally, she spent a minimum of ten hours a day watching and trading the market using a demo account, as she would not risk real money until she felt that she could actually be a successful trader. She stopped looking at trading forums on the Internet because she believed that the winning traders were too busy analyzing the market to answer neophytes' questions on forums. Trading had become a full-time obsession for her. It had become her job, and, like any good professional, she spent ten to twelve hours a day analyzing and tracking the market.

She treated each demo trade she made as though it were with her very own hard-earned money. She rose every weekday morning at five to check the London session to see in what direction her favorite currency pair, the EUR/USD, was headed. Once she got a sense of the market's momentum, she would plan her trades for the day, but she would execute her trades only once the New York session had started at 8:00 a.m. New York time. Jane kept a trading log, where she made highly detailed notes about each trade she took, including the reason she got into the trade in the first place. She also recorded her emotional state when she put on a trade and when she took one off.

Over the years, Jane had learned through watching the market that it had a mind of its own. Trends came and went, and there were long periods in between when the market appeared to have no direction at all. Those were dangerous times, in her experience, because they could tempt the unwary to take trades that had a very low probability of success. In her experience, far too many traders just couldn't stand not being "in the market" for very long, and they would take stupid trades where there was no clear setup. They were just feeding the trading beast within them, the trading beast that gave them the extreme highs when they were on a winning streak and the bottomless pit lows when they were losing. With too many of these traders, winning and losing were secondary to the rush they got from just being in the game and getting some action.

Jane had not allowed herself to fall into these emotional traps. To the greatest extent possible, she controlled her trading. Knowing that the market was a fickle mistress, Jane always made sure that she had at least a 2:1 reward-to-risk ratio working in her favor on every trade she made. She also made sure that she had preplanned and placed her stop-loss and take-profit targets for each of her trades. Most importantly, she never changed her stop loss once she was in a trade. She had seen too many traders change their stop-loss positions and actually increase their risk on a trade once it was going against them. Ultimately, this strategy would lead to much larger losses for them. Jane had steeled herself to adverse market movements once she was in a trade. She knew that over time she would come out farther ahead by just "setting and forgetting" her trade and letting it run its natural course until it hit her take-profit or stop-loss targets.

She was always interested in trying out new trading systems. Jane had purchased many trading books and had attended numerous trading seminars given by so-called experts who touted the absolute invincibility of their systems. And many of them were successful for the first fifty or even the first hundred trades, but, inevitably, these systems would start to break down and become unprofitable. She knew that these systems did not have a large enough number of trades and that they did not have at least two years of trading results to demonstrate the robustness of the system under different market conditions. Jane believed that all trading systems would go through an unavoidable losing period. However, a sound trading system would recover its losses and continue earning profits again. It was similar to an athlete going through a slump, where sooner or later he or she would break out of it because of his or her talent, preparation, determination, and discipline.

She knew that any surefire system could be good for fifty or even a hundred trades and be profitable, but Jane was smart enough to know that it was only when a system had been back tested with at least ten thousand trades that you could place any reliance on it. At the ten thousand-trade level, the law of large numbers would support whether or not a system was a winner. Unfortunately for Jane, she didn't have the computer programming proficiency to implement back testing on different trading systems. She wished that there was a way she could test each system to see if it really worked. This, she thought, would be an awesome project for a computer programmer, who could test a system for ten thousand or more trades. Only then would Jane be able to tell if a system was worth its salt.

Jane had come to the conclusion that any trader should be able to deal with five or ten consecutive losing trades without modifying his or her trading plan or system setup. This was part of the reward and risk characteristics of any manual or automated trading system since risk and reward always went hand in hand. She decided to perform her own experiment. The question she wanted to answer was how many coin tosses would it take to obtain five consecutive tails? What would it take for ten consecutive tails? One coin toss represented one trade, with heads being the winning trade and tails being the losing trade. Through her research on the Internet, she found that the expected number of times you would need to toss a coin in order to obtain five consecutive tails was thirty. It was 1,022 tosses for ten consecutive tails. This meant that she needed to flip a coin only 1,022 times to get this result. This astonished her because most traders start modifying their trading systems or strategies after five consecutive losing trades while there was absolutely nothing wrong with their trading systems. Risk was part of the trading game. One thousand coin flips was not a large number, and yet you could expect ten consecutive trading losses. Similarly, most traders would like to add more filters and conditions to their systems to avoid ten consecutive losing trades; Jane thought they were delusional in doing this because, in essence, they were trying to change the laws of probability, like rigging a coin toss to have more heads.

Jane learned that no one had the market figured out. Sure, someone's theory or trading system might work some of the time, but it sure wouldn't be right all of the time. The market would always outsmart anyone who tried to predict it. So she knew that it was always best to hedge her bets in the event that she had guessed wrong. This was why she always had a stop loss in place to minimize her loss when she was wrong.

The more Jane watched the market and followed the financial news, the more she became aware of the fact that even the most famous economists were never 100 percent certain about their predictions as to where the economy or a market might be going. History might show that they were right in their predictions, but that might take ten or more years to be validated. Economies and markets are not creatures of science whose behavior can be reduced to a set of equations or predictions. Uncertainty will always be present because an economy, and the markets, are made up of people and not numbers. Therefore, human behavior is always the main driver. Jane knew that trying to predict human behavior in any given situation would prove fruitless. However, she also believed that playing the odds when it came to trading the market was an approach that, given enough time and capital, could lead to a profitable outcome.

Jane's strategy included her belief that it was better to lose a little each time she was wrong and to win a lot more when she was correct. Over a long time and a large number of trades, she would have "positive expectancy" working for her. She understood what it meant to cut losses short and let profits run. Jane also made it a habit to calculate the break-even point on each trading system that she came across. As it turned out, she needed to have only a 45 percent winning trade average to break even and a 50 percent winning trade average to generate a lot of profit on systems with high reward-to-risk ratios. She realized that it wasn't necessary to have a high winning-trade percentage to profit. In her experience, she found that few traders understood how to calculate the break-even point on any given trading system, which made it far more likely that they would end up as failed traders.

It seemed to Jane that too many traders focused only on high-probability winning trades without understanding how their average wins and average losses would affect their long-term profitability. Jane had read, and she agreed with the idea, that for a trader to know if his or her system was viable, he or she had to have back tested on ten thousand trades. On top of the back testing, he or she had to conduct at least one thousand live trades before he or she could average his or her wins and losses and have any numbers that were statistically worthwhile. With a live one thousand-trade sample, a trader could rely on the law of large numbers and make a truly informed decision as to whether his or her system worked over the long term. Only then would a trader know if he or she had an edge in trading the market. This was the main reason Jane had not traded with real money—she wanted to collect the results of one thousand real-time trades to determine whether or not she actually had an edge in the market using her trading system. Most traders are drawn into the get-rich-quick mentality; hence, they naively believe that they had an edge in the market after fifty or a hundred successful trades. It was only a matter of time until the law of large numbers caught up to empty their accounts.

Jane was growing tired of the daily grind. She knew that she wanted more from life than simply coming up with a foolproof trading system. There was a big hole in her life that neither trading nor her husband Peter could fill. Call it maternal instinct or just general ennui, but Jane needed something else. Gone was the freshness and excitement of her early trading days, her first discoveries of the market and its promise of untold riches. Gone, too, was the gratification Jane got from learning new trading systems and having successful trades. She needed more in her life. She looked at her two sisters, both of whom had children and happy marriages, and she longed for the same. Though she knew she and Peter would never be able to have their own child, she knew that there was something inside her that called for her to have a child she could love and care for, something to nurture.

That is why Peter's suggestion to adopt a child, which was something he had always been against, couldn't have come at a better time. She would never be at a better place physically and emotionally than right now to take care of a child. She needed this more than anything else in her life, and for the first time, she could really see herself becoming a mother. She would give up her obsession with trading for a while, at least until she and Peter had explored the possibility of adopting a child. That was far more important to her than a trading career. Trading could wait, but becoming a mom could not.

• • •

Like Jane, Joey had stopped trading. He was taking a breather from it after having tanked his trading account for the seventh time in the five years since taking Harry's trading course. That seemed like an eternity ago, and Joey remembered vividly how Harry had made it seem like trading was like stealing money once you learned his techniques. Overall, Joey had lost nearly $250,000 in his quest for financial independence through trading. Every time he had a winning streak, he found himself taking larger and larger trades in the hope of making the "big payday." Unfortunately, his big wins were always followed by greater losses. It seemed like he just could not help himself when it came to trading.

When he was winning, he would increase his lot sizes so that by the end of his current round of trading activity, he was putting 10 percent or more of his capital at risk on a trade. Then, when the inevitable happened, he would lose it all back to the market and more, and he would overtrade recklessly to try to get back at the market. The market didn't care if he won or lost and did as it pleased. Thus, Joey found himself in a downward spiral until he finally lost every dime in his account. At this point he decided that there was something mentally wrong with him, and he sought out help.

He enrolled in a psychology course and took visualization classes. He thought that if he could understand his subconscious motivations that drove him to make reckless trading decisions, he would somehow be able to tame them and become a totally rational trader, removing emotionality entirely from his trading decisions. He had read somewhere that visualization practice was very good for traders, as it could calm them down when they were trading and that this would lead to better trading decisions by putting them in sort of a "Zen-like" state where decision making would come easily.

In his psychology course, he was told that he must learn to accept and embrace risk. That was a good one because Joey always saw himself as a gambler, so accepting risk was never an issue. He could always get out of a losing trade without the slightest emotional discomfort. His problem was not respecting risk enough in his trading. In his visualization classes, he was told that he should see money as a river flowing all around him, and he could take as much as he wanted. He could visualize taking as much money as he needed from the market anytime he wanted. Deep down, Joey knew that this was all nonsense.

He also knew that someone put that money in the market, and in order to take it out, you had to earn it. There was no such thing as a free lunch. It was a big, feel-good thought, but reality was far different. In the end, Joey found that all the psychology and visualization courses in the world wouldn't help him. He also believed that, contrary to what the trading gurus preached to their acolytes, it was false that every loss would put him closer to a win. Joey knew that if he did not have enough trading capital to survive a string of losses, he would not have an opportunity to take advantage of his trading edge, if indeed he even had one.

Being a businessman, Joey was familiar with the concepts of cash flow and contingency funds. A company's sales could be seasonal or cyclic during a year; hence, it had to have enough cash to cover its operating expenses during the slow months. Yet, some of the psychology and trading coaches he encountered had said that he should set monthly goals to achieve consistent growth. Joey knew this was not always possible because there were always good months and bad months, and most couldn't be predicted in advance. Like Jane, Joey observed that trends came and went. There were long periods in between when the market appeared to have no direction at all. It was impossible to have monthly goals because trying to reach them would force the traders to take unnecessary risks. Then there were the coaches who said that he didn't need nerves of steel in trading if he practiced proper risk management.

One of his psychology instructors told him that his emotional issues and limiting beliefs were affecting his trading and that resolving those issues could take years. How was a person going to develop his trading technique if he had to take care of his emotional issues with years of psychotherapy first? This was insane—it was like learning how to ride a unicycle while learning how to juggle three chain saws at the same time. Joey started to realize that trading was a lot more difficult than he had thought.

When Joey was gambling, it was a lot of fun because it provided him with entertaining value. However, trading required him to perform real work. The volatility of his trading account was never an issue for Joey; he could handle a swing of plus or minus 50 percent in his account. Most traders can't stomach such gains and losses. This, Joey thought, was his real trading edge and put him in the top 5 percent of professional traders.

Another trading psychologist told Joey that his problem was in his trading systems, not his mental state. Meanwhile, Joey's private trading coach argued that he needed to work on his trading psychology. He needed to work to overcome his self-sabotaging behavior and limiting beliefs and build genuine values. These lame games of back and forth reminded Joey of a famous Chinese anecdote about a soldier injured by an arrow in a battle. The soldier was brought to a general practitioner, and the doctor sawed off the arrow shaft, leaving the arrowhead inside the soldier's body. The general practitioner bandaged up the soldier's wounds and asked for compensation for his services. The soldier argued that the doctor had not completed his job because the head of the arrow had not been removed. The general practitioner disputed the claim because removing the arrowhead was the surgeon's job. And so it was with Joey—everyone was so specialized that no one was able to provide him with a holistic solution. Joey's famous psychologist had written ten books on trading psychology, and yet he was unable to produce consistent trading results himself.

Another discovery Joey believed he had observed was the value of the herd mentality in the market. In normal times, when the price of something went up, people bought less of it. If the price went down, they bought more. This was how a rational market worked, and this phenomenon was known as the law of supply and demand. However, Joey realized that whenever a bubble occurred, the market became irrational and didn't neatly follow the law of supply and demand. If house or stock prices were going up, speculators would buy more because they believed that prices would continue to climb, which they would as long there was speculative buying. This created the classic case of a self-fulfilling prophecy, which would lead to a market bubble. Inevitably, however, the buying phase would wear out, and a new selling phase would take its place, causing prices to fall back down—how far down was anybody's guess.

The most confusing issue for Joey was trying to figure out when a market had reached its top. There were always the naysayers who would begin calling for the death of any bull market almost as soon as it began. And it is true that whatever goes up must come down, but no one ever knows when that will happen. No one can consistently predict the precise timing of when the market will crash.

Joey investigated the record of some self-proclaimed gurus who predicted the precise crash of the stock markets in 1987 and 2002 based on the Elliott Wave Theory. At first glance, the experts' proclamations looked rather impressive, especially since the Elliott wave had predicted two major stock market events with uncanny accuracy. However, Joey discovered that during the same time frame, the Elliott wave theorists had made forty other incorrect predictions. Their accuracy rate was a mere 5 percent. This made Joey very leery of talking heads on TV shows or elsewhere in the media as well as other predictive systems being offered by market experts claiming to have the ability to call a large market crash or run-up with precise accuracy. Joey knew that statistically there was only a 5 percent chance that they could accurately predict the next event. Unfortunately, the talking heads on the TV shows had selective memories and would only crow about their correct predictions when they all had far more incorrect forecasts.

Joey's biggest problem was with his trading discipline. It was untrue that an average trader can create a mental life that led to internal restraint and that translated into trading discipline. Joey believed that external rules and boundaries were required for effective trading. Joey understood that an average trader could never create the rules required nor have the discipline necessary to abide by them to actually become a successful trader. This is why virtually all companies create operation manuals and policies. Once the rules are established and written down, employees must follow the standard operating procedures, and managers are put in place to make sure that these rules and procedures are followed.

Joey thought that the perfect solution to his trading problems would be for him to have an army of trading robots working for him twenty-four hours a day. This way he could eliminate all trading fatigue issues and any problems with the psychology or discipline of his trading. His robots would always be in the zone. They would not hesitate to put on a trade, even if their last five trades were losers. It would be easier to program the robots with internal rules and discipline than an average trader developing his internal rules. Joey's robots would not load up their positions in an attempt to get back at the market on the next trade. His robots could focus on real trading opportunities and would not perceive them with the nagging sense of pain caused by fear of losing the trade. There would be no problems caused by overconfidence. Joey's army of robots would place no special emotional significance on any trade. Although he did not possess the technical know-how to implement his concept of an army of trading robots, he truly believed that such a system was the answer to ultimate trading success.

When one of Joey's uncles passed away, Joey was needed back in Hong Kong to run the family business. It was a blessing for him, he thought, because then he could go back to Macau and gamble for entertainment. Joey believed that successful FX trading was a pipe dream for any manual trader who was trying to earn financial freedom. Past experience and psychological barriers prevented him from creating a mental life that would lead to internal discipline and then to trading discipline.

Joey looked forward to his weekend visits to the magnificent Macau casinos and the women who were there in abundance. He would let his FX trading go for now, and maybe someday in the future he would create a robotic system to trade. Until then, he thought, he would use his disposable money on the gaming tables of his favorite city.

• • •

Trading continued to consume Arthur's days, even as his son turned five. He had attended many intensive workshops on trading in addition to Harry's advanced classes, and several times he nearly got kicked out for raising a ruckus by challenging the trading instructors. Arthur's instructors would provide examples of where they profited on various preselected trades using one manual trading system or another, which they personally favored. During those moments, Arthur would stand up in class and demand that the instructor produce his or her own trading records so the class could verify that the instructor had actually taken the trade in question. Most of them would come up with an excuse or blame Arthur for disrupting the class.

In North America, it was considered impolite to ask how much money a person made a year, a custom that appeared to Arthur to carry over to trading account statements. The excuse given by the instructors generally was that it was a personal matter and was not to be disclosed. Consequently, many trading gurus took advantage of this custom and represented themselves as successful traders when, in fact, they were not and never had been.

Arthur felt he had had countless moments of enlightenment since he had started learning how to trade, but none of them ever seemed to help him make profits. It seemed to Arthur that he was chasing an elusive dream. He had read book after book on trading—books on options, stocks, FX, and bond trading. He came across many trading psychology books that claimed that once you are able to control your mental state of mind, even if you had a simple or mediocre trading technique, you could still be a successful trader. What a bunch of baloney, Arthur said to himself every time he heard this. Arthur was able to validate that any simple trading strategy would work only for several months and would then fail miserably. Being a brilliant computer programmer, he was able to demonstrate and verify this principle through over ten years of back testing. A simple method would work well during a trending market but would fail during sideways markets or what is known as "choppy" markets in which there is no clear trend established.

Trading requires a flexible strategy that can mold itself according to the market conditions in order to minimize risk, given the overwhelming volatility of the market. The situation is analogous to how certain forms of a car complement different weather conditions. Arthur would imagine himself driving a convertible car, and suddenly it would start to rain hard. By some miracle, the convertible car turned into a sedan with a hardtop. As he drove down the freeway for another ten miles, the weather got worse, and it started to hail and snow. Somehow the sedan turned into a SUV with snow tires, which allowed him to navigate through the dreadful driving conditions. Finally, Arthur got himself to his desired destination and found a small car parking space. Somehow his magical SUV turned into a Smart car, which allowed him to park in the small car spot with ease. This scenario would be a cool trick but one that is not possible in the real world. All the environmental factors in the analogy are comparable to the constantly changing market conditions that every trader encounters. The convertible, sedan, SUV, and the Smart car represent the trading techniques that Arthur would have to choose before he backed his car out of the driveway in the morning.

Most instructors would claim that a trader must use a different trading technique for each type of market. Historical charts showed that a sideways market required a certain technique, while a different technique should be used for a trending market. Unfortunately, none of the instructors could tell Arthur in real time the condition of the present market in which to apply the technique. The bottom line was that Arthur wanted to know the market conditions so he could select the right vehicle before he backed his car out of the driveway each trading day. Trading was the land of hindsight, where the instructors were constantly trying to go back in time to prove what should or could have been, not what would be coming next, and so their advice was worthless.

Arthur would cringe whenever an instructor told him that the market was constantly changing and that he must modify his trading method to go along with it. On the surface, it sounded like good advice, but in reality it was not possible. For example,

Arthur's trading system had been doing well for the past four months, and then he noticed that his system made eight consecutive losing trades. This shift presented him with a quandary. Should he make changes to his trading system now or wait for validation that the market had changed first? If he made changes to his system now, how could he validate that the changes were the right ones for the new market conditions? It would be impossible to make changes constantly on the fly since it would be impossible to validate that the new changes would be suitable for the ever-changing, new market conditions. Arthur imagined that he was trading for a living, which required him to withdraw a certain amount of funds from his trading account to pay for his monthly expenses. If he had no other income and was depending on winnings from his trading account to live on, this would create unbearable stress on him or any other trader. Would he make the change now or next week or the week after? How would he deal with the monthly withdrawals from his trading account that he needed to live on?

There are traders who will never trust any computerized mechanical trading system. They have a fear that the computer will one day take over the world, like in the *Terminator* movies. Some shun the advancement of computerization and believe that discretionary trading is always the best method. Most people do not realize that the first ancient analog computer was designed more than two thousand years ago by the ancient Greeks. The first analog computer was known as the Antikythera mechanism, and it was designed to calculate astronomical positions. It was no bigger than a modern laptop, but it was able to predict both lunar and solar eclipses. Some researchers claim that the device did not really work very well, but these people do not understand the brilliant engineering and concept behind a tool to give planetary positions. The Antikythera device used bronze gear wheels to track the complex movement of the sun, moon, and all the planets. There were more than forty gears, with some sprockets being prime numbers such as 19, 53, 127, and 223. It was a complex and tricky model because the year was controlled by the sun, and the month was controlled by the moon. The time of a new moon was averaging 29.5 days, but this created a problem since twelve lunar months of each year added up to only 354 days. It was eleven days short of the solar year of 365 days, thus causing the natural year with the seasons and the solar year to be out of sync. However, the Greeks knew that nineteen solar years equaled 235 lunar months. This meant that the calendar in the long term would be in line with the seasons.

Another engineering feat was to design a gear that would replicate the moon's movement around the earth. The moon moved around the earth in an elliptical motion, which meant it moved faster when it was close to the earth and more slowly when it was away from the earth. The solution was simply genius. There was a pin gear and slot gear mechanism where the gear with the pin would spin on a slightly different axis compared to the gear with the slot. This adjustment introduced a variability of motion in one of the gears; it plotted the variability of the moon's elliptical motion around the earth. The 223 gear was based on the Saros Cycle used to predict the eclipses of the sun and moon every 223 lunar months. Not only could the Antikythera predict the eclipse a decade in advance, it also could predict the day and hour of both solar and lunar eclipses. More amazingly, it was able to predict the direction of the shadow and the color of the sun and moon during the eclipses. The Greeks used this mechanical system over two thousand years ago to help them determine the planetary alignment. If the Greeks were able to do this twenty centuries ago, one would think that some brilliant engineer could design a similar mechanical trading system to help trade the foreign exchange market with today's technology.

Arthur knew that the mechanical trading system was the solution; however, there had to be a better way in which he could outsmart the rest. What he was starting to envision was a portfolio of automated trading systems, a single trading model consisting of six trading systems (or robots), each of which analyzed the markets from a different perspective. Two models would track up markets, while the others specialized in tracking down and sideways markets. This approach offered greater market insight than single, multipurpose algorithms. Automated, systematic trade initiation would eliminate the delays of trade initiation, a major problem with the older, signal-based, manual trading. Automation would provide a quicker reaction to market changes. The portfolio concept would not attempt to forecast a certain market direction, but instead capture all the possibilities in the market. Many times, Arthur came across trading gurus claiming that trading was a marathon, not a sprint. During the five years since the gang of seven had taken Harry's trading course, nearly all of them had been decimated financially.

Arthur's software concept took advantage of trading opportunities whenever the market presented them at any given time. Only with his automated trading, could Arthur take advantage of these opportunities. Each trade was a "probable fair" trade (one that had an equal chance of success or failure) without the expectation of market behavior. As long as the average losses were smaller than the average wins, Arthur's system would profit in the long run. His automated system's state of mind was not affected by the market's behavior. There was no internal struggle in a computer program.

Arthur's software was constantly in the present moment, and it had the ability to focus on real trading opportunities without the threat of "trader's pain." It did not relate to or remember the last trade, as each trade was statistically independent of every other trade. His system would not hesitate to put on a next trade, even if the last ten trades were losers. It did not load up if the last five trades were winners. When the market provided his system with the preprogrammed trading signal, it perceived the signal with an objective perspective. A subroutine was called upon to execute the trade. It perceived the market as a mathematical probability only. It would trade without fear or overconfidence, while an average trader would take years to achieve such a balanced mental state.

Arthur believed that most manual traders had the tendency to operate out of the fear of being wrong. It would take many years of effort to put one's state of mind at ease to the extent that he or she could enter what he liked to call the "performance zone." Arthur's automated solution would allowed the market and his trading algorithm to be in constant synchronization within the zone. He no longer needed to set up his own internal mental condition or the discipline to stay within this zone. Using an automated trading system meant that there was virtually no likelihood of operating out of fear of being wrong. Arthur believed that anything was possible in the market and that there was nothing for him to avoid. His systematic solution placed the odds of success in his favor by letting the profits run. Arthur understood the laws of probability; he completely accepted that he did not know the outcome of any particular trade, for he knew that over the long run, he would be successful. Automated trading allowed him more methodical profit taking when the market went in the direction of his trades, and it allowed him to predefine the risk and, therefore, cut his losses short. Since all trades have an uncertain outcome and each trade is statistically independent of every other trade, with systematic trading, a trader must commit to a trade and be willing to let the probabilities play themselves out. Each trade is a unique event with an uncertain outcome.

Arthur knew that he had the ability to create such a program; the key was selecting the correct parameters and the right portfolio of trading algorithms. As he knew all too well, the market was constantly changing, and a portfolio of systems would enable him to profit under all market situations. Arthur knew that creating such a portfolio of computer programs was the only sure way to win at FX trading. He would start the development of such a portfolio, and he felt confident that one day he would be able to come up with a bulletproof trading portfolio of systems.

SUMMARY OF CHAPTER 8

1. Get acquainted with the law of large numbers.

Only when a system has been back tested with at least ten thousand trades can you place any reliance on it. At the ten thousand-trade level, the law of large numbers will support whether a system is actually reliable. In addition to back testing, the system needs to have at least one thousand live trades before providing any numbers that are statistically worthwhile. With a live, one thousand-trade sample, a trader can make a truly informed decision regarding whether the system can actually work in the long run. Manual traders must have one thousand live trades to determine whether they have an edge in the market.

2. Risk is a requisite component of the reward equation.

Traders should typically be able to deal with five or ten consecutive losing trades without modifying their trading plan or system setup. This is part of the reward-and-risk characteristics of any trading system, since risk and reward always go hand in hand. Most traders would like to add more filters and conditions to their systems to avoid ten consecutive losing trades, but doing so is akin to manipulating the laws of probability, like attempting to rig a coin toss to have more heads.

3. **Profits can be achieved with 50 percent winning trades.**

A misguided belief adopted by most traders is that more winning trades essentially means more profits. This inevitably prompts traders to keep executing trades until one losing trade wipes out all the profits they have accumulated. When applying a risk-management approach rather than a profit-expectation approach, a 45 percent winning trade average will amount to breaking even, and a 50 percent winning trade average will generate a significant profit. Achieving consistent profits essentially rests on a risk-management approach including consistent lot-size trading, limiting losses, and taking extended (but limited) profits.

4. **Learn to leverage modern tools to assist with your trading.**

The first analog computer was designed more than two thousand years ago by the ancient Greeks. Some of the modern trading tools were not available twenty years ago but are readily available today. Don't fall behind in technological adoption because you will end up falling behind.

5. **There is no such thing as a free lunch.**

It is a fantasy that a trader can simply visualize success in order to take as much money as he or she wants from the market anytime he or she likes. Someone put money in the market, and in order to take it out, a trader must have a trading edge and not a pipe dream. Trading psychologists claim a limiting belief is that reward and risk go hand in hand. Some attempt to turn negative beliefs into positive beliefs; however, the law of reward vs. risk must be obeyed at all times.

6. Consultants often play the blame game.

A trading psychologist will typically blame a trader's problems on the trading trainer and his or her system. The trading trainer will blame the psychologist and his or her program. Between themselves, the psychologist and trainer will blame the trader. If trading psychology and training programs really worked, then we should see a lot more millionaire trading teams with psychologists and trainers combining resources.

7. The market is irrational.

Even trends can be deceiving—as in the case of bubbles (which eventually burst). In a rational market, when the price of something goes up, people buy less, and when the price goes down, they buy more. Whenever a bubble occurs, often driven by herd mentality, prices continue to surge. The trend is not sustainable, and when the bubble bursts, those who set their trading stop loss improperly often suffer greatly.

8. Automated trading is optimal for the FX market.

The currency market does not move only up, down, and sideways—there are whipsaw and many other different transitional markets. Automated, systematic trade initiation eliminates a major problem with the older, signal-based, manual trading technique by helping traders react more quickly to market changes. An automated system does not attempt to forecast a certain market direction, but instead captures all the possibilities in the market. An automated system—proven by sufficient back testing, live trading, and time—brings rationality into an irrational market. Decisions are not affected by greed, fear, outside counsel, trader distraction, or other human factors.

CHAPTER 9

A TAIL RISK EVENT

Harry stared at the ornate ceiling of the hotel suite he and Michelle occupied. It was a grand, old-fashioned room full of exquisite art deco furniture. The bed he and Michelle were lying on had to be at least eighty years old, and Harry wondered to himself how many couples had made love on it. He looked over at Michelle, who was dozing after their prolonged lovemaking session. Her nude body was the picture of feminine perfection with her blonde hair, blue eyes, and beautifully tanned skin that she maintained through regular trips to the tanning salon.

In the nearly eight years since Michelle had first been a student in Harry's trading school, their affair had grown ever more deep and intimate. At first Harry ignored her attention, passing it off as a mere schoolgirl crush. Although he had been attracted to her the first time he laid eyes on her, he didn't allow himself to pursue her, not because he was a man of high principle, but because he was afraid that a romantic fling with a student would ultimately hurt his business. The men would hate him for stealing the best-looking girl in the class, and the women would too because most of them also entertained romantic thoughts about their teacher.

It wasn't that Harry's marriage to Jennifer was bad; it was just that Harry had become bored with his wife. Jennifer was a "good girl" in the sexual sense of the term. She rarely, if ever, took the initiative in bed, and their lovemaking had become routine and all too predictable. Michelle, on the other hand, was the complete opposite. She was always inventing new ways to enhance their lovemaking sessions, and this provoked Harry like nothing else.

Harry first met Michelle right after she had left college when she answered one of his ads to hand out flyers advertising his trading course. She would soon become one of his students as well. She had been just twenty-three at the time, and she had shown interest in learning about trading, thinking that it might provide the financial security that she was sorely lacking. Harry, always generous to any pretty girl, offered her a free lesson. Shortly thereafter, Michelle joined Harry's course at a deep discount in price because she was one of his "flyer girls."

Harry was torn between his desire for Michelle and his need to present a professional image to his students. In truth, he lusted after her, as did every other man who saw her. The day finally came when Michelle asked him to join her for coffee at the local Starbucks, and, in a moment of weakness, Harry accepted. Coffee after class became a regular thing until it graduated to drinks at a local bar. Then one night, after three martinis, both of them took things to the next level. Harry took Michelle to a nearby hotel, and they made love there for the first time.

As time went on, Harry and Michelle developed an amazing relationship. Harry couldn't believe his luck. Not only was

Michelle infatuated with him completely, but the fact that he was nearly twenty years her senior meant nothing to her. Michelle never pressured him to leave Jennifer and marry her. She never asked him for more than what they had, which consisted of working together during the day and in the evening for sex at least three nights a week. The fact that Michelle never pressured him for more was both pleasing and bothersome to Harry. On the one hand, she never asked him for more time than they already were spending together. After all, Harry reasoned, most women would have pressed him to leave his wife and take up living together. This perplexed Harry, but he didn't let it worry him too much. Most of the time, he was just thankful that he had landed such a catch. Men seemed to undress Michelle with their eyes at every opportunity, and this was a huge boost for Harry's ego.

Harry had been in need of a teaching assistant. With the time he spent on administrative work, running the course and the necessary class preparation, Harry had been stretched thin. Michelle was an extremely good student and very analytical by nature. She had taken to reading charts and employing Harry's trading techniques like a duck to water. Additionally, she was a keen student of the markets with an uncanny ability to gauge what was happening in the financial markets and what trends might be in effect. Unfortunately, Michelle was one of those timid souls who found it nearly impossible to put on a trade and, if she did, just couldn't seem to let it run its course. She had an almost pathological aversion to losing money, and she knew that regardless of how well she did her homework in setting up a potential trade, there was always the possibility that it could go bad.

This fear caused her constant mental turmoil. When she did enter a trade, she couldn't just let it play out. At the first sign of a trade going against her, she would close it out (mostly at a loss) and many times would nearly die when she saw it go back in her favor. Trading for Michelle was something that she could do all day long in the abstract, as in a demo account, but when it came to live trading, she just couldn't get over the pain that losing a trade caused her. She knew what she needed to do in any given trading situation, but she just couldn't get past her fear of loss. Harry had suggested to her that perhaps she might think about seeing a counselor because her fear level, at least in his mind, didn't seem entirely rational. Michelle resisted the idea, which Harry couldn't quite understand, since he had tried to take advantage of whatever benefits he could derive by seeking the counsel of several psychotherapists who had treated many traders.

Michelle had seen trading as the opportunity to prove her prowess to the world. This was her original motivation for venturing into this territory, to show the world she had brains on top of everything else. Ironically enough, she found herself typecast in the same role: the hot girl who was used for everything but her brains. Her timid nature paralyzed her trading, so she found herself more successful at pleasing Harry physically than making money off the FX market. She was still proud of herself for going after the opportunity and not remaining in her comfort zone, but the same thought always lingered: would her timidity forever hold her back?

All the same, she had become the best assistant Harry could have ever asked for. First, she was drop-dead gorgeous. This kept the men in class enthralled, and even the women liked having one of their own offering them advice. It gave them a sense of confidence and solidarity in what was typically a male-dominated industry. Second, Michelle was a natural communicator. She had a way of presenting Harry's course material in a way that made sense to even the most skeptical and simple-minded students. Third, she knew all of Harry's trading techniques and proprietary indicators backward and forward. Fourth, she was extremely well versed in the fundamentals of the markets, from the stock and bond markets, to the options and commodity markets, and, particularly, the currency markets. Moreover, she watched most of the financial news shows on cable and kept abreast of the latest market developments online because she loved following the markets and their wild rides. To her, it was like watching a football game or an Indy car race; it was exciting because you never knew from one moment to the next what was going to happen. All in all, Michelle was far better versed in market fundamentals than even Harry, who prided himself on being a financial authority.

Harry used Michelle twice a week on Tuesdays and Thursdays to run his classes. He did this for a reason. Since Harry was selling his students the fantasy that his trading methods would bring them untold wealth, he needed to be able to demonstrate his trading prowess and that his methods actually worked. He tried doing this with a combination of live trading and looks back at prior trades that he claimed to have made. The examples of his old trades were, of course, highly profitable. They were also trades that Harry had never actually taken but had merely selected from historical trading charts that would prove his point. Taking live trades in class in front of his students was a bit trickier to deal with, for there was a better than a fifty-fifty chance that his trades would be losers.

The beauty of having Michelle break up the week for his classes was that she could talk about other things and thereby take the students' focus off of following Harry's live trades on the previous day. This was especially true since Harry never closed out his live trades while he was still in front of the class. Using Michelle as a distraction worked for most students, but there were always a few who kept track of Harry's trading. When he would inevitably be asked about how his trades went, Harry would conveniently say that either he got out of the trade with a small loss if it ended up a loser or that he made a lot of money on it if it went in his favor. There were some students who were smart enough to ask to see Harry's trading account records for substantiation, but he would tell them that he never showed anyone his private trading records as a matter of personal privacy and that he found it rude in that anyone would make such a request.

In the five years since starting his trading school, Harry had become very active in promoting not only his business but also himself as a trading expert. He accomplished this in several ways. He realized early the benefit of networking with members of the professional FX trading community. In particular, he sought out and became friends with many of the FX "gurus" who appeared at the various FX trade fairs and conventions that were held throughout the year around the country. Although he attended at least two trade shows every three months, there were several that he found to be the most beneficial to promoting himself as a speaker—one held in Las Vegas and the other in New York City. Harry realized that speaking in front of a convention hall made up of an audience of newbies trying to get rich through FX was the quickest way to become a name in the industry.

Becoming an FX celebrity was easy for Harry. One of the things he was always sure to do was to socialize with the convention promoters and other top speakers. Harry would take them out on the town, individually or in small groups, where he would pay for all their food and drinks for the evening. Everyone liked Harry, for he was as charming an individual as you could hope to meet, and he found it easy to "con the cons." All he had to do, really, was buy them dinner and drinks at a nice restaurant, and then, if they were so inclined, he would send call girls to their rooms later at night. It was all paid for by Harry, and he, of course, wrote it off as a business expense. The goodwill engendered among the professional FX community was tremendous. Harry was so successful at grooming the FX presenter community that one of the first questions asked when a presenter got to the convention site was "Have you seen Harry anywhere?" Few would even suspect that the vast majority of the presenters were there merely to shill their latest trading system or automated trading robots and that the vast majority of them were, in fact, unsuccessful at trading. They made their money off the sale of their books, courses, and trading systems. Very few of them even traded anymore.

Whenever he was introduced to an audience, Harry made sure to have the emcee tell the crowd that he had helped over ten thousand traders turn around their trading and become successful traders. Of course, there was never any mention of what the terms *successful* or *turn around* meant in that context. Harry's simple money management, proprietary indicators, and trading psychology techniques were touted as the magic bullet for aspiring traders. No one ever asked if Harry had any proof to back up these claims.

All of these presenters were similar to Harry in several ways. First, they showed the audience examples of how their trading had made them millions by using past trades from the charts. The hidden fact was that these trades were selected long after they ran their course and were never shown in real time. This removed all risk that the promoter's system could be proven wrong. Second, these promoters would rarely divulge their trading account records, which, of course, would show that they lost as many times as they won at trading using their unique systems or that, in fact, they never took the trades at all. In some cases, a promoter would actually show a so-called trading account record, but in all these cases the account records had been Photoshopped to show profitability.

Harry knew all the games his colleagues played with unsuspecting new traders. They all knew that the appeal of the possibility of earning unlimited wealth by sitting home in front of your computer was too difficult to resist for most people. This appeal was especially true for people who were in dire financial straits. Since the start of the economic recession in the United States in 2008, the ranks of those willing to give FX trading a try had swollen tenfold. Every year it seemed to Harry that there were more and more fish to catch and fry, and the more the economy headed south, the more this was true.

After several years of running his trading school, Harry realized that by limiting himself to the number of seats his classroom would hold, he was limiting his potential income as well. He took advice from some of the other trading promoters he had become friends with; he decided to offer his course on DVD and create an online trading forum where he would show his trading techniques as they applied to the market. By using YouTube videos, which would direct a viewer to Harry's trading course website, Harry would offer a potential student his home trading course. The course consisted of ten DVDs illustrating the most common types of trading systems, use of Harry's proprietary indicators, money management techniques, and more. What he really offered was the same information that anyone could readily obtain for free by going online to any one of a number of FX brokerage house websites. Nearly all offered similar instructional course information free to anyone who visited their sites.

Harry took advantage of the negative economic news that had been around since the 2008 financial meltdown in the United States. He played on people's fears by saying that they had to look after themselves, and FX was their best answer to economic uncertainty. He told them that the government would not help them and that they could rely only on themselves to provide for themselves and their families. To do anything else was being seriously negligent. He claimed that the US government would go broke because of the insane level of borrowing. The various states were no better with their out-of-control borrowing as well. This approach played well with the personality type that was inclined to look for independent ways to make money. As a group, these people were individualistic, and reliance on government was not something they were inclined to do, as they had little faith in their government's ability to manage its fiscal affairs.

Harry also took a page from the very popular book *The Secret.* This book asserted that if one believed strongly enough in the universe being beneficent and willing to provide to those who believed in its all loving generosity, then he or she would be taken care of. Harry preached the gospel of *The Secret* and that FX trading was perhaps the universe's answer to that promise by providing a way to reach financial prosperity. He cautioned his students not to ask for or focus on the percentage of traders who failed because, by asking about the failed traders, a new student would attract the universe's negative energy, which would consequently doom a new student to failure. Harry told them that it was of utmost importance for a new student to be inspired in order to beat the odds and that by focusing on unlimited financial freedom, they would be attracting the universe's positive energy to help them achieve trading success. Listening to critics or losing traders ranting about their bad FX experiences would inhibit the universe's delivery of the prosperity they were seeking. In essence, he told his members to believe in the universe's generosity and good will. Mixed in with the universal message was the notion that they should believe in his ability to help them become self-sufficient through trading. This is why, Harry told them, it was important to avoid friends and family members who did not support trading for a living as a real profession. The real reason Harry told his students and potential students this was that these people would stop them from signing up for Harry's courses.

Harry charged $395 for his DVD tutorial, but where he made his real money was through his online trading program. For $200 a month, a student could follow Harry and Michelle five days a week working through an analysis of the EUR/USD and the GBP/USD pairs. Harry would mix his market commentary with examples of how he employed his proprietary indicators, trading techniques, and trading psychology. A unique feature of his daily broadcast, which a member would sign into, was that he could also ask Harry questions, and Harry would do his best to answer. Normally Harry's online daily sessions lasted only two hours. Any longer than that and he felt too vulnerable to his members' questions and to the possibility that they would begin to see right through him. To avoid this, he kept his sessions short and sweet.

He would spend a lot of time discussing trades when it was clear what direction they were headed in. If there wasn't any clear trend in the EUR or GBP pairs if they were in a choppy market or if his proprietary trading indicators weren't working, then Harry would jump to the Yen, Swissy, or Aussie pairs, particularly if those pairs were supporting one of Harry's trading techniques. It was an old magician's trick called misdirection. Distract your audience to take their focus off where his system was not working and only show where it worked. As usual, hindsight charts were applied in real time to fool the students. Harry used this technique all the time and made sure that Michelle did as well. There was no chance that his students could pick all the winning trades and avoid all the losing trades when his system was not working. All the winning trades Harry demonstrated were selected with hindsight bias, and losing trades were quickly brushed aside.

He would limit the number of live trades he used in his online trading sessions to one a week each for himself and Michelle. That meant that they had only 104 trades a year that they had to account for to their members. By alternating presentation days with Michelle, Harry made sure that most of the members who were following his trades had lost some interest in the outcome. For the few that continued to keep track, Harry would make up a story about how he got out of the trade later in the trading day if it was going against his initial bet. He would do the same for his winning trades, telling the members he had gotten out at a profit of a hundred or two hundred pips. No one could really challenge him on this as he refused to publish his trading account records, dubbing them "too personal." If it ever really became a critical issue, he could always Photoshop a bogus trading account record, making sure that the name and account number of his brokerage account were blacked out.

Eventually, after about five months of following Harry and Michelle on a daily basis, a member would drop the program and move on. Most often it was to leave FX trading entirely since very few of Harry's students and course members ever ended up making any real money. Most started out with demo accounts, and the smart ones wouldn't even open live accounts, as they never profited in their demo accounts. The one good thing Harry told all of his program members was that they should not trade live until they had at least three months of profitable demo trading. Very few ever made it. As for Harry's 104 trades per year, it was nowhere close to the statistical sample of one thousand live trades needed to demonstrate statistically a true trading edge in the market. Harry had done the math, and it would take one of his students ten years to figure out that Harry had no edge in the market. In his heart of hearts, Harry knew that 90 percent of his students would give up trading within three years, and none would actually follow him consistently over the ten-year period required to expose the secret that his system was essentially worthless.

The turnover in Harry's online program didn't bother him in the slightest because there were always new people who signed up every month. In fact there were more people signing up than dropping out, so Harry continued to make money. Since going online, Harry had kept a steady membership of over one thousand members, with each paying him $200 a month. He was making nearly $200,000 a month. His expenses, including Michelle's salary, amounted to only $30,000 a month, so he was almost literally raking it in. Not bad for only a couple of hours work a day, he thought.

Over time, Harry became something of an FX market guru. He had established a network of influential trading friends to such an extent that he would often be asked to join panel discussions on network news programs where he would be seen by millions of people. Like clockwork, after his appearance on one of these shows, the number of hits on his YouTube videos and his website would jump dramatically, which would ultimately lead to more members for him. As a result, Harry made sure that he appeared on as many TV shows as possible. TV appearances translated directly into increased sales, and Harry loved the respect and admiration he got from the other financial "experts" he shared the stage with. He was finally feeling like the market heavyweight that he had always aspired to be.

• • •

With his daily meditation back on track, Ron was ready to resume his trading activities. He was now in a better mind-set to face the markets after having been tormented with the unpredictability of the FX market. He had also experimented with just about every type of trading system and was now using a number of real-time trading signal providers, which were subscription services that he paid thousands of dollars to every month. At first, these signal systems seemed to work very well. His first month using them he had gains of about 20 percent on average. His second month was down a little from his first at 14 percent. However, at the end of his third month using these systems, he was a negative 3 percent overall. This inconsistency made him crazy as he could not for the life of him figure out what was going wrong.

In speaking with a representative of one of these signal firms, he learned that their signal service, like virtually any other type of trading system, was prone to moving in cycles. It had periods of ups and downs. This representative also told Ron that he had observed a fairly common trading phenomenon. When their system was doing well, they would get a big influx of new customers. But after six months, the system would start losing fairly consistently; with the signal system becoming unprofitable, the firm's customer base would drop. Then the cycle would start all over again. When subscriptions were lower, the system seemed to become more accurate, and the inevitable happened—new customers piled on.

After speaking with other knowledgeable trading experts, Ron learned that all trading systems will go through a losing or underwater period. An underwater period would contain both the drawdown period and the recovery period. Risk and reward went together, even with signal systems. However, most signal followers were always attempting to defy the statistical probabilities by picking a trading system that would continue to win forever. Ron figured out that the best way to decide whether to use any system was to get in when it was bottoming out. This meant beginning to use it when the system was well into a losing period and not when it was winning. He did not want to select a losing system to start trading, but instead to select a trading system that had done well over a period of several years but was currently going through a drawdown period. It was rather counterintuitive, but it made perfect sense. Ron learned that a good trading system is one that can demonstrate its profitability over a period of several years. Since it had a long enough track record, it had proved itself to have an edge in the market. It was only a matter of time before the system's trading edge would reappear, based on favorable market conditions. Ron's analogy was that of a star athlete who was underperforming—sooner or later he would break out of his slump. The old Wall Street adage to "buy low and sell high" was never truer.

Unfortunately, new system subscribers make several rookie mistakes, such as selecting the most profitable trading system, even if it has less than twelve months' trading history. Subscribers pile on to the most profitable system, hoping that their profits will continue to rocket upward. What they don't understand is that with huge returns come huge risks and that a system's past performance with a short track record is based primarily on luck and is not likely to be repeated over the long term. Most subscribers don't allocate a long enough time commitment to a trading system. They have the tendency to jump from one trading system to another, hoping by some miracle to get onto the winning train each time. Subscribing to a trading system is similar to investing in an athlete. You can't trade your athlete whenever he or she has a bad game. You also can't expect him or her to score the winning goal at each game. Most subscribers have a myopic view and unreasonable goals for their "athlete." The bottom-line question is whether the athlete has performed well overall for the season. Most signal subscribers should look at the overall performance of their system for the entire year and not just each monthly result. To be successful, they must be fanatic about a system and commit to it with great loyalty. If a subscriber does not understand the philosophy of the trading system he or she is using, then he or she should not trade with it. Picking a trading system is similar to picking a business partner; it is important to stick with him or her in the good times as well as the bad.

All trading systems are prone to cycles that typically move up and down. This is not a fallacy; it is simple physics. Risk and reward are omnipresent companions. In order for a trading system to generate rewards, it must take on risks. Losing periods or underwater periods are inevitable, and there isn't a system that is immune to them. Most traders, however, make the assumption that if a system starts out profitable, it will always remain profitable, without taking the notion of risk and reward and cycles into consideration. They will join a system when it is profitable with the expectation that the streak of profits will continue forever. Reality then checks in after a period of six months when the system starts experiencing consistent losses. This is all part of the cycle, and, in keeping with the cycle, it will begin to see profits again once it has gone through the underwater period.

Traders who are consistently profitable are fearful when others are greedy and greedy when others are fearful. They don't automatically assume that their system is a winner because it has provided a string of wins during a winning period. Nor do they declare the system a failure just because they experienced losses. They look at the bigger picture and understand that a trading system performs similar to a pro athlete. Even the best athlete will go through a slump but eventually will return to his or her top performance. Choosing a system requires more than just reading reviews; one has to consider when to join the system. If you truly want to know whether your system is a winner, join the trading system when it's losing, and look at its long-term performance. In trading, it is always about the gestalt.

Ron also came across another trading system outfit that claimed it had hired some of the most successful FX traders in the world. All of these traders were vetted with the company's proprietary screening process, which included verifying their trading success history. The company's VP was trying to convince Ron that it was easier to have his account mirror the trades of these traders. Whenever they made trades in their own accounts, the same trades would be copied onto Ron's account instantaneously, saving him the time and effort of manually placing the trades himself. Ron was quite impressed with some of the gains achieved by these traders because they each had over twelve months of trading results with more than a 1,500 percent gain. Being a member of the gang of seven, Ron knew the stories of Charlie's and Joey's outrageous gains—each of which only ended in disaster. But still curious, Ron pressed hard and found out from the VP that the traders at the firm started out with their accounts funded at only $250 and by luck turned it into $4,000. In a couple of cases that number was even more, resulting in the aggregate return of 1,500 percent. Ron questioned this company's strategy because a trader can trade aggressively with $250 and lose it all, as $250 was not a lot of money. However, in Ron's case, losing a million dollars by duplicating the trades of a high-risk trader did not make any sense at all. Imagine if that trader went from $4,000 down to $2,000 for a 50 percent loss. If Ron had followed those trades, it would have resulted in a loss of $500,000. This firm had sourced $20 million in venture capital money to promote its system using the same strategy it tried to use on Ron. Ron was looking for only a 25 percent return per year on his $1 million account, and he was not interested in the 1,500 percent return that was aggressively marketed by the VP of this particular firm. He could only shake his head in dismay at how truly gullible and stupid the public could be. They deserve to lose their shirts, he thought to himself.

• • •

Arthur had been working on his automated trading system for eight years and had spent the last two years testing it live, and he was making great progress on his system software development. His system was becoming more and more refined each month as he continuously made new discoveries on the best way to apply his algorithms to FX trading. Arthur continued to do his research on market dynamics and read all the books he could find on the subject. His library of trading books was fast approaching five hundred, and he was running out of space to store them all. But with each new book he read, the more he became convinced that over 90 percent of the authors of these books didn't really have a clue as to how to approach the market in a way that would consistently generate profits. Nearly all of them were just repeating the same old tired trading system ideas that, in Arthur's opinion, would ultimately lead the hapless trading newbie to a cleaned out trading account.

Arthur knew that for the brand-new trader, the learning curve was horribly steep. It took professional traders years to learn how to trade and even then most of them were only marginally successful. Arthur remembered seeing a statistic in the *Wall Street Journal* once that shocked him. The article recounted an analysis of the profitability of the big investment banks' currency trading departments, which concluded that most made only a 1 percent to 3 percent annual profit. These were institutions at the top of the financial pyramid, with all the resources available in the world, including proprietary trading algorithms created by the most brilliant minds in mathematics and computer science. If these premier financial institutions could do no better than a 1 percent to 3 percent edge, how could the newbie possibly hope to make any real money from trading?

Arthur was a certifiable genius in his own right. He had gone to the best technical schools, where he had studied mathematics and computer science and was always at the top of his class. He felt he could hold his own with anyone in these areas, especially as they related to creating trading algorithms. He knew that if he could perfect his systematic trading system, he would have a product that would give the new trader a footing equal to the big boys.

Arthur's systematic trading solution took the hindsight bias contained in virtually all trading indicators and discretional manual systems out of the equation for the beginning trader. By presetting entries and exits automatically, Arthur's system removed the decision dilemma all new traders faced: whether or not to pull the trigger. Arthur's system was designed to act without input from the account owner/trader at all. In fact, Arthur knew from his two years of live trading that the system worked best if not interfered with. Over 95 percent of the time when he experienced a losing trade, it was because he stepped in and tried to manage the trade better than the system. However, Arthur knew that traders, particularly new ones, would want the ability to intervene in their trades, essentially taking over the trade from the trading system. Although Arthur knew from experience that this was foolish, he made sure his system would allow a trader to step in and take over the trade from the algorithm. He believed that as a trader became more familiar with his system, his or her confidence in it would grow to the point where he or she would step back and let the system do the job it had been designed for. Once this stage of confidence had been reached, the trader would start to see real profits accumulating, and this would reinforce Arthur's advice to just let the system do its job, which it could do better than the trader ever could.

Most trading systems, even automated ones, were never successful over the long term because they were based on mathematical formulas that relied on input from the market and would generate a certain output based on that input. The problem with this approach was that any market is just a collection of individual traders. Since the markets are really nothing more than a reflection of thousands of individual opinions on what direction the markets should be going in at any given point in time, they were also reflections of the collection of the many different environmental and emotional states of the traders in those markets. That being the case, no market is ever the same twice, and being able to project forward what direction it will go in is nearly impossible.

Arthur's system was very different from the other systems he had seen. He had built in a predetermined stop loss and take-profit targets for each trade setup that his system identified. If the "take trade" criteria were met under his system's rules, then it would place the trade. Once in the trade, the system's predetermined stop loss and take-profit targets would manage the trade. The beauty of Arthur's system was that it would manage its trades without emotion and without any reference to past trades it had taken. This removed the biggest impediment of manual trading: human emotion. In Arthur's experience, it was almost impossible for a human trader not to be affected by his or her past trading performance, either good or bad. This emotional element would cause most traders either to get out of their trades too soon or stay in them too long. Ultimately, emotions would lead to a losing trade.

Arthur's automated trading system, however, was governed by the laws of mathematical probability, not human emotion. His system was designed to generate profits if it was left alone and given a long enough time period. It didn't make any difference to Arthur's system if its last ten trades were losers or winners; if the setup criteria of the algorithm were met, the trade would be put on and managed according to the predetermined system criteria. This criteria was what Arthur had spent so many years trying to formulate and refine. All of his system parameters had been based on his statistical probability formulas.

Arthur's system needed only a 50 percent winning trade percentage to be profitable. This was because he had made sure that each trade's stop-loss placement was much smaller than its take-profit target. He had selected a 2:1 ratio of take profit to stop loss, and this guaranteed him profitability. By removing human interference in the trading process that was surely governed by emotion instead of probability analysis, his program assured success over the long run. This was in line with the Taoist philosophy of action through inaction. This profound and ancient Chinese insight claimed that the universal force in all things was always at work and for the good. It was only when man interfered with its operation that things got screwed up. Accordingly, if one followed the Tao (translated as "the path"), a good and harmonious outcome would be achieved. For Arthur, his system was the trading Tao, and if the trader left it alone, it would bring him good fortune in the end. If the trader intervened, it would lead to a distortion and, ultimately, a bad experience for him. As the old Taoist saying went, "Sitting quietly, doing nothing, spring comes and the grass grows by itself." The beauty of Arthur's system was that it allowed the trader to do just that, sit quietly.

The human mind is a remarkable tool for several reasons, one being its ability to identify its own limitations and then create ways to make up for it. Technology, in virtually any form, is simply man's way of getting over the hurdle of being human. But it all starts with someone's genius—that is, without brilliant thinking and innovative minds, none of the technology that we so heavily rely upon would be created. As the world continues to grow, both in population and via the growth of ideas, we begin to recognize more ways in which technology can assist us. One of the ways humans can employ innovative thoughts is in the FX industry. Here's an industry that is becoming ever more complicated and competitive. Traders who are serious about keeping up in this fast-paced industry and developing an edge that will help them create consistent profits need more than quick thinking; they need the option of employing virtual intelligence when need be. Technology is not to replace humans, but to assist us. Whether that is through efficiency, accuracy, consistency etc., there are numerous ways computers can make the task of trading easier.

Traders who combine their own knowledge with technology are often more relaxed and more focused. This state of mind gives them a substantial advantage in an industry that so often gives birth to anxious, worried traders who are so fearful of making a mistake that even their high IQs are not enough to overcome their anxieties. A trader who works with technology is a smart trader. As the world becomes technologically advanced, those who are equipped with the intelligence to build, understand, and/or make use of this technology are the ones who get ahead. Consider eras before machines when brawn beat out brains; the heavily muscled man who could work long hours was an asset and had the advantage. Fast-forward to today, and humans still require an advantage or edge, except now we value intelligence significantly more, and it's the ability to put a machine to work (rather than work like one) that garners respect. Computer-assisted trading offers a number of benefits to traders, without compromising their own intelligence. The trader still has control and is able to interject when he or she wishes. Rather than simply relying on one mind (his or her own), the trader now has two forms of intelligence that can help make consistent, profitable trades.

Arthur had spent more than eight years perfecting his system, including two years of demo account trading on the final software revision of his program. He had borrowed $150,000 from family members and friends to start trading with it and get his system into commercial operation. Arthur believed that by demonstrating positive results with a sizable trading account, he could persuade more investors and potentially large hedge fund managers to use his software. Arthur knew that Singapore, London, and New York spent hundreds of millions of dollars each year hiring the best software developers, like himself, to design the ultimate trading programs. It was through Arthur's hard work, pure obsession, unrelenting determination, and perseverance that he finally had something to compete with the brightest trading minds in the world. He had spent many years and thousands of hours giving his blood, sweat, and tears to his system's development. Now he had reached the point where he finally felt he had figured out the market. But the market had one final lesson for him to learn.

Arthur had been trading with PFG Best for nearly eight years and had the utmost confidence in them. This brokerage was one that did not play all the silly, manipulative games that the average retail FX brokerage did. Additionally, Arthur had a personal friendship with the chairman and CEO of the company. It came as a cruel surprise and shock to Arthur when he read in the newspaper that PFG Best had filed for bankruptcy. Arthur had developed a system that he felt was bulletproof. The weak link in his chain was one he never thought about: the brokerage house he used to support his trading system. As it turned out, Arthur's account, as well as those of all his clients, had become worthless overnight. This put Arthur out of business immediately. It seemed the market had had the last laugh, and it was on him.

SUMMARY OF CHAPTER 9

1. FX celebrities are not always to be believed.

A credible reputation ideally takes years to develop, but shrewd networking and relationships with opinion leaders can create credibility overnight. A lot of the so-called FX experts have cunningly managed to create an aura of credibility that is nothing more than a facade.

2. Trading trainers may employ the trick of misdirection.

Misdirection is a tool used by trading trainers to distract their audience to take their focus off where the system was not working and show only where it worked. In a live trading forum, a trainer will quickly dismiss where the system is not working and quickly demonstrate another currency pair where it does work. In reality, these are hindsight charts that were applied in real time to fool the students.

3. It is important to have the right balance of positive and negative thinking.

Always allow yourself the opportunity to question others. An overemphasis on one's strength will lead to weakness.

Don't let others use the excuse that only positive thinking attracts positive results. Many will attempt to use this excuse to take advantage of you and prevent you from questioning the potential pitfalls.

4. **A good system demonstrates profitability over the long term.**

The performance of a system cannot be gauged if it has not been trading for at least two to three years and, therefore, conducted an adequate number of trades. A long track record helps prove that a system has a sustainable trading edge and that any profits it made were not a result of sheer luck. The factor of time gives prospective users the confidence that the system will perform well under different market conditions.

5. **Question any claim of extremely high returns. Demand proof.**

Ask to see actual trading statements, and don't accept excuses. Some of the largest, most established currency trading institutions that have seemingly all the resources in the world generate returns of less than 7 percent over time. Anyone claiming 1,500 percent per year should be written off as gambling and unsustainable returns.

6. **Frequently moving from one system to another is a recipe for failure.**

In FX trading, one must consider a medium-term horizon of three to five years. Many investors are quick to withdraw their capital when their returns do not support a perpetually increasing trend. It has been proven that investors who hop from one fund to the next, chasing performance, tend to do vastly worse than those who abide by the trading strategies they have adopted from the start. A winning process requires commitment, patience, and loyalty.

7. **All trading systems will experience losing periods.**

Risk and reward go hand in hand. In order for a trading system to generate rewards, it must take on risks. Neither manual trading nor systematic trading systems are immune to these up and down cycles. It is important to know both the maximum equity drawdown in percentage and also the maximum underwater period of a trading system. The underwater period contains both the drawdown period and the recovery period. The maximum equity drawdown defines the minimum capital investment, and the underwater period determines the duration of commitment to a trading system.

8. Automated trading offers an edge.

Automated trades are managed without emotion and without any reference to past trades. Automated trading removes the biggest problem with manual trading: human emotion. It is almost impossible for a human trader not to be affected by the past trading performance, either good or bad. The emotional element in trading causes most traders either to get out of their trades too soon or stay in them too long. An automated system replaces emotion with mathematical probabilities and, in effect, removes a paralytic barrier to trading successfully.

CHAPTER 10

MARKET WIDOW-MAKER

Night had fallen, and the glare of flashing police lights pierced the darkness. Outside Harry's office, a small army of police and TV news crews lined the perimeter of the office building. Inside Michelle was duct-taped to a chair, her mouth taped shut. In front of the boardroom's large, exterior window, Harry knelt with his arms and wrists taped; he was not gagged. Standing over Harry was his old student Charlie.

Charlie had a 9 mm Beretta semiautomatic pistol in his right hand pointed at Harry's left temple. Charlie had screamed at Harry for over an hour, to the point that he was becoming hoarse. He had lost his entire life savings trading FX, and he turned his anger and rage on Harry. Charlie was now destitute. Having lost his full-time job eight years before and thinking that he would be able to support himself through his trading, he took, and later relied upon, Harry's FX trading course.

Trading seemed to Charlie to be a new, life-changing career and the door to fortune. He thought that he could work anywhere in the world. He thought he would have the freedom to work as little or as much as he wanted so that he would have time to devote to his love of movies and cooking. Charlie wanted to take control of his financial future and to do it from the comfort of his own home. Harry had sold him on the idea that trading was about developing a lifelong skill that would give him the life he always dreamed of—a laptop by the pool or on a beautiful, sandy beach overlooking an emerald ocean, with coconut trees swaying gently in the pleasant breeze—an image that he relentlessly envisioned. The reality was that the currency market was highly volatile; spending just minutes a day in markets that are active twenty-four hours a day and making decisions often fueled by greed or fear was a sure route to disaster. He loved the wild rides the market took him on, from the emotional peaks of the highest highs and the valleys of the deepest lows he had ever experienced. Since taking Harry's trading course, Charlie had become a true trading addict, watching the market during most of his waking hours. As a result, his life had become very limited and ultimately unbearable. Aside from his trading, he left his computer screen only to make runs to the store for groceries and other necessities. He never saw his friends anymore, though he never really had many to begin with.

Charlie was the "quiet loner" personality type that fit the description of every deviant ever profiled in the news. His family members, those who were still talking to him, had been unable to make any meaningful contact with him in the past few years. They had given up inviting him to family events, even Thanksgiving and Christmas. When someone in the family did happen to catch Charlie on the phone, he was always abrupt and cold with them. He was not someone you wanted your kids around, and he certainly was not fun company at a family party. There was just something not right about Charlie, and his family had begun to worry to the point that they had openly discussed holding an intervention for him with a trained professional. His sister contacted several intervention specialists, and each one told her that it sounded like Charlie had had a psychotic break and needed help right away, which caused the family even more anxiety and concern. The problem was that they couldn't reach a consensus about going forward. None of them wanted to make a move without all the family in agreement. No one wanted to be the only intervention advocate, and so Charlie was left to fester.

Charlie's sister now found herself standing in front of Harry's office building talking to her brother via a cell phone and surrounded by police officers monitoring the conversation. She had been coached by the officers on how to persuade Charlie to stand down. She was called by the police to come to the scene to try to talk Charlie out of his plans. Nothing she said appeared to make the slightest bit of a difference to him. He maintained his position, holding the gun on Harry in full view of the police, reporters, the live webinar audience, and his family members. The police hostage negotiator, a man who had been involved in over a hundred hostage situations, also failed to sway Charlie. Time was running out, and the decision to use a sniper to kill Charlie before he could do harm was shaping up to be the only resort. A police sniper was in position, just waiting for an order to fire after reporting to his superiors that he had a clear head shot. A decision had to be made soon, and it was agreed that if Charlie didn't surrender in the next ten minutes, the order would be given to execute him.

• • •

Charlie had broken into Harry's office around eight that night and came across Michelle. As soon as she saw the look on his face, she began to scream, but he came prepared and immediately gagged her with a sock and covered her mouth with duct tape. He quickly duct-taped her wrists behind her back so she couldn't put up a struggle and led her to the boardroom, where he taped her to an office chair directly in front of the window that faced the street outside. After securing Michelle, Charlie set out to find his real target: Harry. He knew Harry was in the office because he had been following his movements for the past six weeks and knew every step he took every moment of the day. When Harry left his house, Charlie was in his car waiting to follow him, which he had been doing every day from early morning until Harry returned home at night. Only when Charlie felt that Harry had settled in back home for the night, would he go back to his place to get some sleep. Following Harry had become an obsession, and Charlie knew his every move from Harry's house, to his office, to the hotel rooms where he was joined by Michelle. At times Harry and Michelle would have their sexual liaisons at the office. Charlie wondered if Jennifer knew that Harry was cheating on her. He really didn't care and felt no sympathy for her; after all, she was being well provided for off Harry's ill-gotten money. He actually felt jealousy when he learned that Harry was having an affair with Michelle. Like all the other males in their group, he was also infatuated with her. Charlie had never met a woman like her. He hadn't even known a woman like her existed outside the movies. That Harry had managed to lure Michelle into his arms further enraged him.

That night, Charlie was certain that Harry was in the middle of his infomercial webinar trying to convince more naïve people into taking his "life-changing" trading course. Just thinking about Harry's sales pitch, Charlie became more infuriated. The course did actually change his life, but in the worst ways possible.

Harry was in his office presenting the webinar via his laptop as Charlie barged into the room. With the gun pointed directly at his chest, Harry froze in shock and disbelief. Charlie started screaming unintelligible sentences and gestured for Harry to lie facedown on the floor. Harry complied, still in disbelief that it was all actually happening. Charlie then duct-taped Harry's hands and arms behind his back and then helped him get off the floor. It was Charlie's intention to catch Harry during the middle of the webinar so that he could let the world witness his former teacher's fall from grace. Grabbing the laptop, Charlie then led Harry to the boardroom, where Harry saw Michelle bound and gagged. Her eyes pleaded with Harry not to do anything stupid that would put their lives in further jeopardy. Harry didn't need much convincing. He was hardly the hero type and was totally out of shape, a victim of the good life he had achieved over the years.

Multiple 911 calls were placed to the local police. It seemed that everyone was watching the live hostage situation on his or her computer. It was live drama, like the O. J. Simpson car chase in Los Angeles many years before. The operators immediately relayed the information to police dispatch, and three squad cars were sent to the scene. The officers on the scene couldn't believe that there were already several broadcast TV vans and crews set up. They thought that someone at the police station must have been taking bribes from a reporter. What the police didn't know was that an audience all over the world was watching the live broadcast on their computers instead of the TV.

Shortly after the police perimeter was set up, central command called in a hostage negotiator and a SWAT sniper team. The negotiator's first step was to establish communication with Charlie. The negotiator called Harry's boardroom number and started his attempt to calm Charlie down to a point where he could be reasoned with. The negotiator requested that Charlie close the laptop because the webinar was still being broadcast live worldwide. Charlie threatened to kill both Michelle and Harry if the police cut the Internet or disrupted the webinar. Charlie wanted Harry to confess his trading scam to the whole world and to belittle him in front of everyone.

The police captured the conversation between Charlie and Harry in an official transcript.

Charlie: "You've destroyed my life. You and your FX trading ploy. "

Harry: "Um, how did I ruin your life?"

Charlie: "I took your trading course, and you made me and all the others believe that all we had to do was follow your advice, and we would make all the money we wanted."

Harry: "I never guaranteed anyone would make money, ever. That's something you read into what I was saying."

Charlie: "You made us all believe that we could become rich by trading! You said there was the potential for virtually unlimited upside when we traded consistently. You sold us dreams and lies and knew at the back of your mind that it was bullshit."

Harry: "Hey, if you're not making money trading, that's your fault. I've seen students make the same mistakes over and over again. They don't do their homework, and then they get into trouble and blame me. There's nothing wrong with any of my methods. They're tried and true. Anyone who knows FX trading will tell you that. Look, killing me won't solve anything. Please calm down, and let's just—"

Charlie: "You liar! You're just another trading criminal. Where are your results? You show me now, or I will blow your head off right here!"

Harry: "Okay, look, trading is hard, and I may have inadvertently simplified it. Most traders either don't stay in a trade long enough to see it through to a profit, or they hang onto a losing trade far too long."

Charlie: "Oh, really? Now your conscience wakes up, and you decide to speak the truth? How many trades have you even made in the past three years? Did you even have a break-even point?"

Harry: "I don't know. I don't remember."

Charlie: "How 'bout I crack your head open? Maybe then you'll remember."

Harry: "Okay, okay, over a hundred trades—seventy percent winning. I don't know what you mean by break-even point."

Charlie: "What's your average for winning and losing trades?"

Harry: "Average? Twenty pips winning trades and eighty pips losing."

Charlie: "That shows you minus a thousand pips and losing money."

Harry: "I…I meant average sixty pips losing trades."

Charlie: "You're still losing money, yet you claim to have a great trading system. You can't even lie to save your own life. You are truly unbelievable."

Harry: "I never claimed that I personally had a great trading record. It's not my fault you guys assumed I did. I didn't guarantee anyone that they would be successful. You're all so greedy, you didn't care that the odds have always been stacked against you—you all thought you were the exception to the rule because you're such smart little snowflakes. Well, now you know better, and it's your fault, not mine!"

Charlie: "Fuck you. You promised us you'd teach us everything we needed to know about making money. You told us we could learn to trade the market profitably for the rest of our lives. You regurgitated the same tired lies every day. You made me lose my entire life savings. I'm totally broke, I have no job, and now no one will hire me."

Harry: "You're where you are today because of your own mistakes. It's none of my doing. I can't be your babysitter and tell you what to do on every trade you make. So shoot if you're going to shoot—otherwise, fuck you!"

Charlie: "Fuck it. My life is over now, and so is yours, asshole!"

The next sound heard over the speakerphone was a single shot from Charlie's pistol, and Harry immediately crumpled to the floor like a puppet whose strings had been cut, dead. The police sniper didn't wait for the kill order and took his shot. The .308 Winchester full-metal-jacket bullet struck Charlie in the center of his forehead and splattered his brains across the room. Like Harry, Charlie was killed instantly, and his lifeless body fell over Harry's. Student and teacher joined in a final death embrace, two more victims claimed by the market widow-maker.

• • •

When it rained, it poured. Arthur lost his job at the facial-recognition software company due to the bad economy. He was totally broke and deeply in debt after the debacle with his brokerage house going bankrupt. He knew that his system was exceptional and capable of making outstanding returns. He also knew that those returns would never be realized if he couldn't find the capital to get it off the ground. Now he was $150,000 in debt, mainly to family and friends, and the shame of it was killing him. It was one thing to owe money to a faceless institution like a bank, but when it is your parents, brothers, sisters, and best friends, it was excruciatingly shameful. This is what hell must be like, Arthur thought.

He had no job and, therefore, no money coming in to support his wife and eight-year-old child, much less to relaunch his business. He literally didn't know where he was going to find the money to pay his next month's rent. He hadn't told his wife about his job loss and had no idea how to deal with this debacle.

He pondered taking the chance that his company's closing wouldn't be reported on the local news where she would find out anyway. He couldn't go back to family and friends again, and a bank would never lend him the money because he had no collateral and no income source to support the repayment of a loan.

It was late one night when Arthur was trying to get to sleep, and he thought about Ron. He and Ron had been in the gang of seven, and the two of them got together a couple of times a year to swap stories. Arthur sensed that although Ron was very rich, he didn't have many friends. Whenever Arthur called him, Ron always seemed sincerely overjoyed to hear from him. Maybe he could get financing from Ron, Arthur wondered. After all, Ron was the only one of Arthur's acquaintances who had the kind of money and business acumen that could resurrect his business. Arthur made the mental note to call him first thing in the morning.

The next morning, Arthur got Ron on the phone as he was driving to one of his many McDonald's franchises. Arthur suggested that they get together for coffee and that he might have a business proposition he would find interesting. Ron agreed to meet his old friend the following afternoon at their usual coffee shop. Arthur had used the day before the meeting to come up with a pitch that would appeal to Ron. Surely once Arthur had gone through the ins and outs of his automated trading system, Ron would see the tremendous potential and want to join him as a partner to relaunch his venture.

Eight years ago, this coffee shop had been the gang's favorite hangout. There used to be so much energy, liveliness, discussion, and laughter and much debate on the potential to strike it rich with FX trading. The group members would exchange stories and lessons they had learned and would egg each other on to improve their trading results. Those magical and happy moments were now gone, and, instead, a sense of sadness filled the place, sadness for what might have been. It seemed to Arthur that the atmosphere was now more like a funeral for the disbanded gang of seven, and Ron's and Arthur's visit was more like a tribute to their fallen comrades.

They both saw the continuing coverage of the incident between Harry and Charlie, but neither of them really wanted to talk about it. It was pretty clear what had happened and what the motivations were. They both agreed that Harry, like so many other trading instructors, had oversold his products and services. It was the classic example of selling dreams to poor souls who were looking for a way out of their financial woes by appealing to their greed. It had taken Ron and Arthur eight years after their initial training course with Harry, many years of trading battle scars, plus tens of thousands of dollars in trading losses and multitudinous additional training courses, books, and seminars to become even remotely successful traders. Trading instructors were basically selling balloons: large and grand on the outside, but hollow on the inside.

Only now, after all these years of struggle, did they feel like they had graduated from their trading apprenticeship. Up until his untimely demise, Harry was still sucking in new traders looking for that magic path to untold wealth. Had Harry been truthful, he would have told his students that it would take five to ten years of commitment before one could become even remotely successful at trading. Of course, if Harry had been honest, he would never have attracted any students. Harry may not have been guilty after all, since he was merely playing the rules of the game.

Ron and Arthur felt terrible for Charlie. This was a guy who had bought into the dream and paid an awful price for it. He had lost all of his life savings and ultimately his life. Both Ron and Arthur knew that life's big lessons were not about success or failure but how you pick yourself up and start over after a major failure. Although to the outside world it looked like Charlie had failed at the picking himself up lesson, maybe he had succeeded in a fundamentally important way with a final contribution to society by trying to obtain the confession from Harry of the truth about trading. It might have been worth it if even one unsuspecting person avoided the trading trap after hearing about Charlie's story.

Did Harry deserve to die? Probably not, but he would continue to run his scam for the next twenty years and mislead thousands more people. Did Charlie purposely to take a life that night or did he just want to produce a confession? Was it in the heat of the moment, similar to many impulsive trading experiences felt by new traders when they pull a trigger on a trade? There were many unanswered questions, and, similar to a whipsaw price pattern on a chart, people can only speculate and alter facts to explain after the event had happened. But no one could really know what was going through Charlie's mind that night.

It was good to see his old friend again. For whatever reason, Ron felt a kinship with Arthur that he didn't with the rest of the gang of seven. Perhaps he saw himself in Arthur. They were both entrepreneurial and very creative, each in his own way. Ron respected Arthur and recognized his genius. He had never met anyone with Arthur's IQ and ability to grasp complex concepts so quickly and surely. That was perhaps another reason why he liked Arthur so much; he respected and admired his intellect.

After twenty minutes of getting caught up on what had been going on in their lives, Arthur began his presentation, including all the details of what had happened to his business venture and the mountain of debt he had accumulated. Arthur also told Ron how ashamed he felt about owing his family and friends so much money and that he had no conceivable way of repaying them. Ron sat there and listened intently as Arthur told his story, keeping his questions to a minimum. Then Arthur delved into the trading model he developed and the potential it had to cause a dent in the trading landscape. Arthur described it as a disruptive technology that would revolutionize trading because of its progressive and futuristic edge that capitalized on the strengths of the currency market and allayed some of its weaknesses. Ron, having firsthand experience in FX trading, understood where Arthur was coming from. He could relate to most of what he was saying. After Arthur had finished, Ron took a few moments to digest what he had heard. The entrepreneur that he was, he saw an opportunity and knew that opportunities like this cannot be waited on. Otherwise, someone else will grab them. The technology developed by Arthur had colossal risk attached to it because automated trading would raise considerable apprehension from the general public. A machine handling my millions of dollars? But then again, the rule commonly attached to trading actually originates from business: with greater risk, comes greater reward.

Ron told Arthur he would consider buying all the rights to his system for $500,000 cash. That would be more than enough to take care of Arthur's debts and support his family for a few years. However, Ron had several conditions to this offer. One was that Arthur would run the new venture, with Ron providing the necessary capital to make sure that it got going and became profitable. Ron said that though he knew the fast-food business and considered himself a pretty decent FX trader, he knew nothing about program engineering and automated trading systems, nor did he have the knowledge that Arthur did about how to market it. Those things, the actual R&D and day-to-day operations of the business, he would leave to Arthur and would step in only when major decisions needed to be made.

The second condition was that Arthur had to agree to a non-compete clause that would prohibit him from starting or being involved in any way with another automated trading system for a period of seven years. Arthur would receive a salary of $100,000 a year and a bonus of 10 percent of all net profits the new firm generated at the end of each fiscal year. Additionally, Ron would offer Arthur an equity "earn-in," whereby if the business hit certain profit targets, he would earn a predetermined percentage of the equity of the firm up to a 30 percent overall cap.

Arthur couldn't believe his ears. His old friend had come through for him in a way he could not have imagined in his wildest dreams. Not only would he be able to pay off his debts and pay everyone's interest on their loans, but he would have immediate money to provide for his wife and son for the next few years. The best part, though, was that he would be able to stay a principal of the business and run it with little interference from Ron, and he had a very generous compensation package as well. Though he wouldn't be the sole owner, he had a chance of earning a good deal of his business back if his system performed as he projected. He really couldn't have asked for a better deal.

For his part, Ron thought that if even half of what Arthur told him was true, the new venture would be generating millions in profits annually within five years. All this for the modest investment of $500,000. He would also be helping a friend. This was a win-win situation for both of them, he thought. Ron was starting to feel excited again, just as when he first started trading and had seen the potential that it offered. The next day Ron instructed his lawyers to prepare the documents for his deal with Arthur. He also had a computer systems engineer review Arthur's program to ensure its viability, and the report he got back was that the system did indeed seem to be as Arthur described it. That was enough for Ron to hear, and on Friday of the following week, he and Arthur met in his lawyers' offices to sign the deal, after which Ron handed Arthur a check for $500,000. Arthur had tears streaming down his face as he hugged Ron and thanked him for his faith and trust. Ron took Arthur and his family to the most expensive restaurant in town, where they had the best meal of their lives. Arthur never felt happier.

Ron, however, had no grand pretensions about his new business. Unlike so many newbie traders, he didn't expect to make 400 percent profits a year. If he could make 25 percent a year on his investment, like he did on his McDonald's restaurants, he would be very happy. He knew that he, like all traders, had limited abilities, but after studying and trading the FX market for years, he had learned at least a few things that should keep him more grounded and wiser.

He would fund the new venture up to $10 million, which—if he could get a 25 percent return—would mean he would be earning $2.5 million a year. This amount was the same as his McDonald's business was making him annually, and that was the benchmark he would use to gauge his new company's performance. By setting a limit on the potential gain of his new venture, Ron was setting a limit on his risk. Going on what Arthur had told him about the automated system, this seemed doable. Time would tell, but he would not fall into the trap of expecting mammoth returns, as so many beginning traders did. He would build the venture up slowly at first and then, over time, ramp it up to see if it might make more than a 25 percent return. If it didn't, he would still be satisfied. After all, how many investment vehicles provided a 25 percent annual return? Ron could think of none.

He knew that a successful trader was one who was highly motivated and who worked hard at perfecting his or her skills. He himself had spent untold hours reading everything he could on the FX market and trading strategies. He had blown through numerous trading accounts his first five years of trading, and it was only the last few years that he made a small profit. The one reason that he could see as an explanation for being successful was that he had deep pockets, which was his trading edge. None of the other gang of seven members had that luxury. They had never been able to make it through to the point where they had paid their dues to the Market Goddess and were allowed entrance to her realm.

Ron thought of his classmates. Joey was very smart and good at math and, hence, could figure the odds quickly on each trade. This ability had come from his gambling background. That was his edge. But Joey also lacked the discipline required of an experienced trader, just like a typical gambler, and ended up too many times just taking a crapshoot at a trade, which would inevitably lead him to a losing trade. Jane was resilient, but she didn't have the stamina and commitment to achieve greatness in trading. She had the devotion, the discipline, and the focus to get over the learning threshold to become a proficient trader. She found that in order to be a great trader, she would have to give up too much of her life. She wanted more than just the rush that trading provided. She wanted to start a family and become a mother. Michelle was very intelligent and analytic. She was the best analyst of the group. However, she lacked confidence and could not deal with the fear of failure. She was paralyzed by overanalyzing trades, a classic case of "analysis paralysis." Her problem was that when it came to placing a live trade using real money, she froze up. She couldn't stand the thought of making a losing live trade. That was her fatal flaw. Arthur was a bona fide genius. When it came to math, probability analysis, and computer science, Ron had never met anyone like him. But genius wasn't enough, Ron thought. One needed capital in sufficient quantities to be able to make trading or any other type of business work. Arthur's story was a classic case of what happens to an undercapitalized venture. The slightest error, in Arthur's case his brokerage's bankruptcy, and he was out of business. The same held true for beginning traders. Most didn't realize or chose to ignore the fact that they needed to start their trading with a sufficiently big trading account to weather a string of losses. This was Ron's edge, his ability to take a string of losses and keep in the trading game. None of his former classmates had that ability, which was why only he would be a successful trader in the long run.

When Ron got back home that evening, he was in a contemplative frame of mind. He had been going over what it took to make it as an FX trader. He pulled down from the bookshelf his latest trading journal and began writing the following:

Qualities of a Successful Trader

1. At least one thousand live trades to establish the trading edge
2. Stamina, both mental and physical
3. Ability to multitask

4. Good at math
5. A highly intelligent and structured mind
6. A personality that thrives on fast-paced activities
7. The ability to take losses in stride
8. The ability to pull the trigger on trades
9. Confidence without overconfidence
10. Resiliency
11. A portfolio of trading systems
12. The ability to live a balanced life
13. Extreme discipline in dealing with the market
14. The financial resources to withstand the losses the market dished out until you become a proficient trader
15. A disciplined focus on risk management, not profit making

The list went on for more than fifty items, but the only one that Ron circled and highlighted was "money, lots of money." He truly believed that with his deep pockets and Arthur's systematic trading solution, they could satisfy all the necessary qualities. He felt sorry for any new traders who were going up against the market without the arsenal of trading edges that he and Arthur had.

Ron had many more ideas floating around in his brain that he wanted to incorporate into the business, but that was for another day. He was tired, and it was time to go to bed. As his head hit the pillow, he let out a deep sigh of contentment and once again felt the tingle of excitement in his stomach. He couldn't wait to wake up the next morning and get going with Arthur on their new venture. How exciting life could be, Ron thought, as he drifted off to a deep, restful sleep, the first good sleep he had enjoyed in many months.

EPILOGUE

Ron and Arthur's business, CTS Forex, continues to grow. Their system has performed consistently and successfully due to the use of multiple models and a risk-management approach to trading. Each of the six trading algorithms the system uses views the markets from a different perspective—two evaluate uptrends, two monitor downtrends, and two examine markets that are moving sideways. The robots trade on statistical probability, not trends, fundamentals, or technical indicators. The risk-management approach calls for cutting short losing trades and allowing winning trades to hold and achieve a specified gain greater than the specified loss amount. Using this approach, the system has to pick correctly only 45 percent of the time to break even and 50 percent of the time to achieve a sizable profit. Live trading of more than three thousand trades over a three-year period has shown an annualized of more than 30 percent return on investment.

With the success of his models, Arthur has become a frequent source of information for publications and services such as the *Wall Street Journal*, *FX Trader Magazine*, and Dow Jones. The client base of the company has expanded dramatically. When the models were first introduced, the client base was almost entirely individual traders, but as the models have proven themselves in the market, wealth advisors, FX portfolio managers, and financial institutions are all using CTS Forex models.

Winsor Hoang (Arthur) lives in Vancouver, British Columbia, and may be reached at winsor@ctsforex.com.

FX trading involves substantial risk of loss and is not suitable for all investors. Past performance is not indicative of future results. Data are provided for informational purposes only and do not constitute investment advice.

SOME FINAL THOUGHTS

In reading these adventures in FX trading, readers will, of course, want their favorite character—or the one who resembles them and their trading habits most closely—to come out on top. They may also like for all the traders to find some way of succeeding because the industry tries to delude us into thinking this is possible. What readers must understand above all is that the industry is not for everyone.

A trader is a type. Successful trading requires a specific personality as well as an edge that will help one overcome the inherent perils of this practice. The average trader is fearful, greedy, undisciplined, overenthusiastic, and limited in terms of capital. All these shortcomings work against traders, and they are extremely difficult to overcome. Even if traders can develop a strong mindset, their capital may still limit their ability to obtain consistent profits. Likewise, traders may have wealth on their side, but their fear and lack of discipline can hold them back.

The ideal trader is willing to limit his or her reward to 25 percent a year. Risk and reward go hand in hand; hence, with lower reward, there is lower risk. The average person will not be satisfied with 25 percent per year on a $10,000 account because he or she can't live on $2,500 per year. A wealthy person, such as Ron, is happy with 25 percent return per year on $1 million because he can easily live on $250,000 per year.

Readers may wish for an "average" person to become the top trader, but the reality is that most average traders will fail because they strive for unrealistic goals, such as turning a $10,000 account into $1 million. Even with a 35 percent return per year, this goal will take sixteen years to achieve. If the account starts with $100,000 at a 35 percent return, it will take half the time.

In addition to using his or her wealth, the ideal trader applies technology to his or her trading habits. He or she understands that being human is a disadvantage in the market because no amount of psychological training can rid him or her completely of his or her fear and emotions. Also, despite being intelligent, he or she may not have the necessary discipline. Technology, on the other hand, works with traders. It is always disciplined and has no emotions. Traders who use the advancements of technology, or who have the IQ to create the technology, have a true edge in the FX market.

ACKNOWLEDGMENTS

This book would not have been possible without a great deal of help from many people. I would like to take a moment to express my deep gratitude to everyone who took time to review this book and make recommendations.

I would especially like to acknowledge Thomas Craig. He asked all the right questions and helped me organize my thoughts. Without his assistance and support, this book would not have come out in the form it is now.

A special thank you to Adelaide Kwaning for her wonderful suggestions and unique insight. You persisted in the review of the manuscript while enduring the pain of battling bone infections. I will forever be indebted for your unwavering support. You are a fighter and an inspiration.

Dick Monroe, thank you for your resolve in getting me to change the book's subtitle. You have been extremely kind and generous with your time in helping me with my many endeavors.

Mo Saïd, thank you for your positive encouragement and your inquisitive attitude in learning more about trading.

Next, I would like to thank my loving family. My brother, Winn Hoang, and his wife, Lynne Dang. You are a source of strength and wisdom for me. Beth Lau, thank you for all the helpful input and critique.

Finally, a very special thank you to my wife, Lisa Lau, for understanding how much this project means to me. You inspire me to share my knowledge and relate inspirational stories. My one percentage genius was marrying you, and my 99 percent perspiration is making you happy for the rest of your life.

Winsor

DISCLAIMER INFORMATION

Before deciding to participate in the FX market, you should carefully consider your investment objectives, level of experience, and risk appetite. Do not invest money you cannot afford to lose.

US Government Required Disclaimer: Commodity Futures Trading Commission. Futures and options trading have large potential rewards but also large potential risk. You must be aware of the risks and be willing to accept them in order to invest in the futures and options markets. Don't trade with money you can't afford to lose. This book is neither a solicitation nor an offer to Buy/Sell futures or options. No representation is being made that any account will or is likely to achieve profits or losses similar to those discussed in this book. The past performance of any trading system or methodology is not necessarily indicative of future results.

CFTC rule 4.41: Hypothetical or simulated performance results have certain limitations. Unlike an actual performance record, simulated results do not represent actual trading. Also, since the trades have not been executed, the results may have under-or-over compensated for the impact, if any, of certain market factors, such as lack of liquidity. Simulated trading programs in general are also subject to the fact that they are designed with the benefit of hindsight. No representation is being made that any account will or is likely to achieve profit or losses similar to those shown.

The information contained in this book is provided with the objective of "standardizing" trading system, and is intended for informational purposes only. It should not be viewed as a solicitation for the trading system. While the information and statistics given are believed to be complete and accurate, we cannot guarantee their completeness or accuracy. As past performance does not guarantee future results. No part of this document should be considered apart from the Disclosure Statement contained herein.

Winsor Global Financial Inc. and Winsor Hoang do not guarantee the adequacy, accuracy or completeness of any information. Neither Winsor Global Financial Inc. nor any of its respective affiliates, officers, directors, agents and employees make any warranty, express or implied, of any kind whatsoever, and none of these parties shall be liable for any losses, damages,or costs, relating to the adequacy, accuracy, or completeness of any information on this book.

Any opinions, news, research, analyses, prices, or other information contained in this book are provided as general market commentary and do not constitute investment advice. CTSForex.com, Winsor Hoang, and Winsor Global Financial Inc. are not liable for any loss or damage, including without limitation, any loss of profit that may arise directly or indirectly from use of or reliance on such information.

- Completely automated systematic FX trading
- 3,000+ non-high frequency trades over 38 months
- 1percent fixed stop loss and 2.6percent fixed take profit
- Statistics & probability trading not fundamental nor technical analysis

The Bull, the Bear, and the Baboon is not a how-to guide for FX traders. It is a collection of experiences of a group of people who became known as the "Gang of Seven." They were part of a group who enrolled in the course of an internationally known FX trader and trainer. By reading about their actions, observations and experiences, the reader will gain a much better understanding of the odds a potential FX investor faces.

It's not an exposé. But it does offer insights into how those new to the foreign exchange markets run into trouble. And, from their experiences, it offers lessons on how to avoid those traps and mistakes that cost 90 percent of those who trade foreign currencies to ultimately lose money.

From their experiences came a philosophy and a course of action—CTS Forex. Readers should put aside the unrealistic dream of near-instant wealth. And they should disregard the thought that one must make a correct trading decision more times than an incorrect decision to generate a respectable return.

The FX market is the purest form of market. It is huge. It is international. The news that affects it is immediately available to all. Because of its size, there is virtually no chance for manipulation. And it is unpredictable.

In 2004, we at CTS Forex began developing a systematic trading solution that disregards fundamentals, overlooks trends, and concentrates instead on statistical probability. Because the software automatically trades using risk criteria set by the client, it is not affected by emotion, time, or market movements. It is pure analytics in a pure market.

Because this is not an instructional guide to FX trading, we would like to share with you thoughts that have come from the Gang, CTS Forex developers, and our clients.

On emotion in trading:
Greed and fear often lead to costly mistakes. Applying automated technology to trading, profitable opportunities are acted upon immediately and the discipline needed to secure and retain profits is enforced.

Learning—paying one's dues:
Experienced traders acknowledge that an amateur doesn't become a successful professional until at least ten thousand hours of practice have been achieved. No new trader should expect to effectively compete with seasoned professionals.

Overcoming the learning curve:
A reliable, successful, automated trading system offers the new FX trader the benefit of others' learning and a competitive advantage over the professionals who manually trade.

On the claims of "experts":
Whether they teach fishing, cooking, or foreign exchange trading, the teacher may be understanding and sympathetic to one's concerns. But if the student fails, in the teacher's eyes, it is due to the student's failure to follow instructions—not the instructions themselves.

Timing and patience:
The successful grower understands that a tree needs time in order to bear fruit. It must survive the cycles of good and bad weather. Like the fruit

tree, FX can provide a steady harvest of profits. And, like the tree, the harvests will come over time, not all in the immediate season.

On profit and loss:
The wise investor inherently knows that losses should be cut—unemotionally and consistently. And profits should be allowed to run. Consistently employing this discipline, one need not be right every time or even fifty percent of the time to succeed.

Money management:
Seasoned professionals know that risk management is not about the 1 percent or 2 percent risk per trade but is based on the overall total account drawdown. Being able to tolerate twenty consecutive losing trades is expected, and it is not a tail-risk event.

Computer as a tool:
From the abacus to the handheld calculator, from the Excel spreadsheet to an automated systematic trading solution, by embracing the proper tool, we benefit from its efficiency, discipline, and the trading edge it offers.

THE SYSTEMATIC TRADING SOLUTION

Failing to profit from personal lessons taught by many internationally recognized foreign exchange trading experts, Winsor Hoang, founder of CTS Forex and a member of the "Gang of Seven," reflected upon the realities of FX trading and the practical lessons learned the hard way. He understood the following:

> *The market is unpredictable. Certainly some trends take place, but day-to-day events are the key factors in volatility. And volatility represents opportunity.*
>
> *Technical and fundamental analysis are time-consuming and rely upon trends. Trends exist, but even the smartest FX trader can be wiped out in a trending market.*

> *Manual, signal-based training frequently misses or is too late to profit from an opportunity. No person can monitor the international markets twenty-four hours each day.*
>
> *It is difficult for manual traders to maintain discipline when their money is at stake. Emotions lead to rash decisions. Those who regularly gamble generally lose not only their accumulated profits; they also lose their initial investment.*
>
> *Computer models that employ only one analytical method of evaluating the market fail to accurately evaluate the differing conditions—up, down, and sideways markets.*
>
> *Long-term consistency in trading is the key to profitability. Nothing is more consistent and systematic than computer-assisted FX trading.*

Adhering to these principles and employing the skills of some of the best mathematical minds available, Winsor Hoang went to work on the development of an automated FX trading system. Seven years later, after thousands of live trades, the models were stable and ready for market. Since 2010, CTS Forex has consistently provided returns that eclipse the Dow Jones Index.

INTRODUCTION TO CTS FOREX

In May 2010, after seven years of development, testing, and cash trading, CTS Forex released its software for investor use. Although past performance is not indicative of future results, the performance of the CTS Forex system is apparent after more than 3,000 non-high frequency trades over 38 months. Each trade is placed with 1percent fixed stop loss and 2.6percent fixed take profit. Our average hold time is twenty-four hours, and our maximum hold time is two weeks. The potential return on investment is much greater than the return on investment from a Dow Jones Index benchmark.

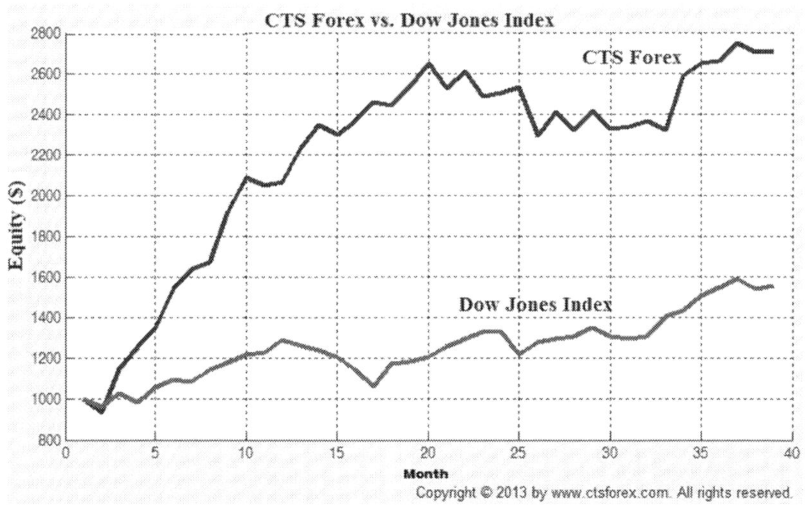

PAST PERFORMANCE IS NOT NECESSARILY INDICATIVE OF FUTURE RESULTS. FOREX TRADING IS COMPLEX AND CARRY A RISK OF SUBSTANTIAL LOSSES. THEY ARE NOT SUITABLE FOR ALL INVESTORS. THE ABILITY TO WITHSTAND LOSSES AND TO ADHERE TO A PARTICULAR TRADING PROGRAM IN SPITE OF TRADING LOSSES ARE MATERIAL POINTS, WHICH CAN ADVERSELY AFFECT INVESTOR RETURNS. THE INFORMATION CONTAINED IN THIS BOOK IS PROVIDED WITH THE OBJECTIVE OF "STANDARDIZING" TRADING SYSTEM PERFORMANCE, AND IS INTENDED FOR INFORMATION PURPOSES ONLY. IT SHOULD NOT BE VIEWED AS A SOLICITATION FOR THE TRADING SYSTEM. THIS IS A MODEL ACCOUNT IN REAL TIME UNDER ACTUAL MARKET CONDITIONS. SPREAD, EXECUTION, AND SLIPPAGE WILL VARY FROM BROKER TO BROKER.

Many FX traders and computer-assisted trading models premise their actions and activities on consistently beating the market—leveraging, varying lot sizes, and making a high percentage of winning trades. The trading models used in the CTS Forex system perform differently; as a result, they need only 45 percent winning trades to break even and 50 percent winning trades to produce the results depicted above.

CTS FOREX'S SYSTEMATIC STATISTICS

Risk management is a key element of the CTS Forex computer-assisted trading process. Consistency and discipline enforced by the models reduce the potential of loss. Although an investor may override the system at any time, comparisons of CTS Forex returns to manual and semiautomated trading systems consistently reflect the superiority of CTS Forex both in return on investment and consistency of gains.

3-Year Statistics 1

www.ctsforex.com Yearly Risk Free: 1% Yearly Target: 5%

Absolute Return Measures	
Average Monthly Return (%):	2.84
3 Month Return (%):	1.7
6 Month Return (%):	16.7
12 Month Return (%):	12.3
Total Return (%):	170.1
Average Monthly Gain (%):	5.5
Average Monthly Loss (%):	-3.71
Compound Return (%) Monthly:	2.65
Annually:	36.9

Absolute Risk Measures	
Standard Deviation (%): Monthly	6.2
Annually	21.5
Gain Standard Deviation(%):	18.1
Loss Standard Deviation(%):	8.3
Downside Deviation(%):	2.57
Semi Deviation(%):	3.9
Skewness:	0.85
Kurtosis:	4.21
Maximum Drawdown (%):	-13.4
Drawdown Period (months):	7
Recovery Period (months):	10

PAST PERFORMANCE IS NOT NECESSARILY INDICATIVE OF FUTURE RESULTS. FOREX TRADING IS COMPLEX AND CARRY A RISK OF SUBSTANTIAL LOSSES. THEY ARE NOT SUITABLE FOR ALL INVESTORS. THE ABILITY TO WITHSTAND LOSSES AND TO ADHERE TO A PARTICULAR TRADING PROGRAM IN SPITE OF TRADING LOSSES ARE MATERIAL POINTS, WHICH CAN ADVERSELY AFFECT INVESTOR RETURNS. THE INFORMATION CONTAINED IN THIS BOOK IS PROVIDED WITH THE OBJECTIVE OF "STANDARDIZING" TRADING SYSTEM PERFORMANCE, AND IS INTENDED FOR INFORMATION PURPOSES ONLY. IT SHOULD NOT BE VIEWED AS A SOLICITATION FOR THE TRADING SYSTEM. THIS IS A MODEL ACCOUNT IN REAL TIME UNDER ACTUAL MARKET CONDITIONS. SPREAD, EXECUTION, AND SLIPPAGE WILL VARY FROM BROKER TO BROKER.

3-Year Statistics 2

www.ctsforex.com Yearly Risk Free: 1% Yearly Target: 5%

Absolute Risk-adjusted Return Measures	
Sharpe Ratio Monthly:	0.48
Annually:	1.65
Calmar Ratio (3 years):	2.77
Sterling Ratio (3 years):	2.6
Sortino Ratio Monthly:	0.94
Annually:	3.27
Omega Ratio:	3.02

Relative Risk Measures	
Beta:	0.18

Relative Risk-adjusted Return Measures	
Alpha:	2.61
Treynor Ratio:	15.6
Jensen Alpha (3 years):	2.55
Information Ratio (3 years):	0.78

Tail Risk Measures	
Value at Risk (99%):	-11.7
Modified Value at Risk (99%):	-8.15
Expected Shortfall (%):	-14.6

PAST PERFORMANCE IS NOT NECESSARILY INDICATIVE OF FUTURE RESULTS. FOREX TRADING IS COMPLEX AND CARRY A RISK OF SUBSTANTIAL LOSSES. THEY ARE NOT SUITABLE FOR ALL INVESTORS. THE ABILITY TO WITHSTAND LOSSES AND TO ADHERE TO A PARTICULAR TRADING PROGRAM IN SPITE OF TRADING LOSSES ARE MATERIAL POINTS, WHICH CAN ADVERSELY AFFECT INVESTOR RETURNS. THE INFORMATION CONTAINED IN THIS BOOK IS PROVIDED WITH THE OBJECTIVE OF "STANDARDIZING" TRADING SYSTEM PERFORMANCE, AND IS INTENDED FOR INFORMATION PURPOSES ONLY. IT SHOULD NOT BE VIEWED AS A SOLICITATION FOR THE TRADING SYSTEM. THIS IS A MODEL ACCOUNT IN REAL TIME UNDER ACTUAL MARKET CONDITIONS. SPREAD, EXECUTION, AND SLIPPAGE WILL VARY FROM BROKER TO BROKER.

Sharpe ratio (annually) ≥ 1 = good, ≥ 2 = very good

Calmar ratio ≥ 1 = good, ≥ 3 = very good

Sterling ratio ≥ 1.5 = good, ≥ 3 = excellent

Sortino ratio ≥ 2 = good, ≥ 3 = very good

Beta < 1 = investment has less volatility than the Dow Jones Index benchmark

Alpha > 1 = investment has outperformed the Dow Jones Index benchmark

Treynor ratio ≥ 1 = good, ≥ 5 = excellent

Information ratio ≥ 0.5 = good; ≥ 1 = very good

ABOUT THE AUTHOR

Winsor Hoang is the founder and CEO of CTS Forex, an automated, statistical, risk-managed FX trading system that produces substantial profits with just 50 percent winning trades. Winsor learned currency trading the hard way after enrolling in a number of supposed experts' FX training courses around the world. Applying the experts' fundamental and technical techniques, he lost most of his investment. Winsor remained convinced currency trading offered great opportunity—if one could manage risk and the role emotions played in trading.

Using engineering and statistical expertise gained from his undergraduate studies at the University of Victoria (BSEE/honors) and fifteen years working with high-tech companies such as Nortel Networks, RIM, and Sierra Wireless, Winsor began development of fully automated systematic trading models. He based the models on TradeStation, Ninja Trader, and MT4 and MT5 trading platforms. In 2010, after seven years of development, testing, and trading his own money, he introduced CTS Forex to the market. Winsor has nearly two decades and more than twenty thousand hours of trading experience. His automated FX trading system continues to produce consistent returns, regardless of market movements.

CTS Forex provides a trading edge for high net worth individuals and currency fund managers wanting to diversify their portfolios and increase overall portfolio returns. CTS Forex trading models track and analyze the foreign exchange markets and initiate trades based upon investor-established risk profiles.

Clients establish risk and trading criteria consistent with their goals and then select the appropriate trading model. A trading model employs six trading subsystems, each of which analyzes foreign exchange markets from a different perspective. Two subsystems track up markets, while others specialize in tracking down and sideways markets. This approach offers greater market insight than single, multipurpose algorithms.

CTS Forex is actively working with several high profile mathematicians, statisticians, computer science and computational finance specialists at the University of Calgary to create new analytical models for both FX and commodity markets.

A SPECIAL OFFER FOR READERS

Thank you for investing your time and money in this book. I hope that it has been helpful in understanding the promises, pitfalls, and, most of all, the profit potential of FX trading.

For traders who buy and read his book, I invite you to our periodic, free Computer Assist Trading webinars. To join us, simply enroll using the link below. In these webinars, you will have the opportunity to learn about setting a risk profile, choosing a modeling system, and automated trading. You will also have the opportunity to pose any questions that you might have about trading and investing.

Please register now at www.ctsforex.com/bullbearbaboon.html.

CTS Forex also provides investors, free of charge, investment tools and training at www.ctsforex.com. These include the following:

- Money management advisor. *NEW* Determines optimal initial trading capital based upon investment profile, reward/risk preferences, and winning trade percentages. Downloadable and free.
- Investment performance statistics. *NEW* Generates different investment risk and risk-adjusted statistics with a simple text file input. Downloadable and free.
- Benchmarks of the best FX brokers based on empirical data, not peer reviews.
- System validation correlating back testing with forward testing.
- Recordings of Winsor's video FX training.
- Platform tutorials for MT4 and MT5 platforms.
- E-mail notifications of live online seminars with Winsor Hoang.

Offers are subject to change without notice.
Sincerely,
Winsor AGA Hoang

Made in the USA
Charleston, SC
24 September 2013